Against Photography:
Early Works 1975–1990
Ian McKeever

imprint

Against Photography: On the dialectical method of Ian McKeever
Mark Prince

'the test of a first-rate intelligence is the ability to hold two opposed ideas in the mind at the same time, and still retain the ability to function'
F. Scott Fitzgerald, 'The Crack-Up'[1]

As they are viewed from a greater remove, the disjunctions with which artistic movements succeed one another tend to betray underlying continuities which were not apparent at the time. Early conceptual art of the late 1960s and early 70s was a reaction against the last manifestations of modernist orthodoxy still lingering at the end of the 1960s. Adopting pragmatic forms which had previously been considered anti-artistic, such as text, photography, and performance, the conceptualists posited an objective art, which, by inference, qualified formalist abstraction as decorative and solipsistic.

It is ironic, therefore, that early conceptual art now appears to have been among the last manifestations – along with US Minimal Art – of 20th-century modernism's categorical purpose; its attempt not merely to qualify the art of the past, but to erase and reinvent it with new tools and new means; its investment in the innate value of now; and its tendency to produce artists that come in groups, with a common purpose shared among their like-minded peers. An ambivalence between rejecting the modernist past and conforming to it fits the historical position of early conceptual art on a cusp between late modernism and the postmodern relativism which succeeded it.

Emerging from a context in which modernist painting and sculpture was being superceded by conceptualism, Ian McKeever's art of the 1970s and 80s is remarkable in attempting to juggle painterly abstraction and conceptual art. Instead of striving to resolve this contradiction he transmuted it into a dialectical model which would give onto a series of others,

as though in its image: between painting and photography, belief and reason, abstraction and representation, logic and intuition. True to the conceptual, relativistic side of this equation, McKeever's art of the 1970s embodies a conception of an artistic practice as a space accommodating conflict and doubt which later generations would consider threatening to the coherence of a single, artistic position and even an artist's functional self-identity. In the context of market-driven, early 21st-century contemporary art, in which an artist is considered to be a marketable brand which should appear as resolved and singular in purpose as possible from the moment it is presented, it is salutory to perceive the trajectory of McKeever's early work admitting the irreconcilability of coexisting positions as an ongoing rather than resolvable condition.

McKeever's career splits on either side of a personal and artistic break at the end of the 1980s. This is more than an arbitrary narrative convenience; it is a fulcrum around which his development pivots. At the end of that decade, the dialectic between alternative forms of representation, which had hither-to characterised his art, was set aside. Photography, to which he had assigned an increasingly marginal role since the middle of the 1980s, was relinquished. In an interview in 1990, on the occasion of his mid-career retrospective at the Whitechapel Art Gallery in London, McKeever spoke of wanting painting to be 'strictly of itself'. He was not merely adjusting priorities but foregoing a dialectic between different modes of representation as the central theme of his art. Painting had not merely won out over photography. A model of art ultimately deriving from modernist abstraction had prevailed over the conceptualist model which had challenged it.

Drawing for proposed
'grass verge painting'
for a wood, July 1975

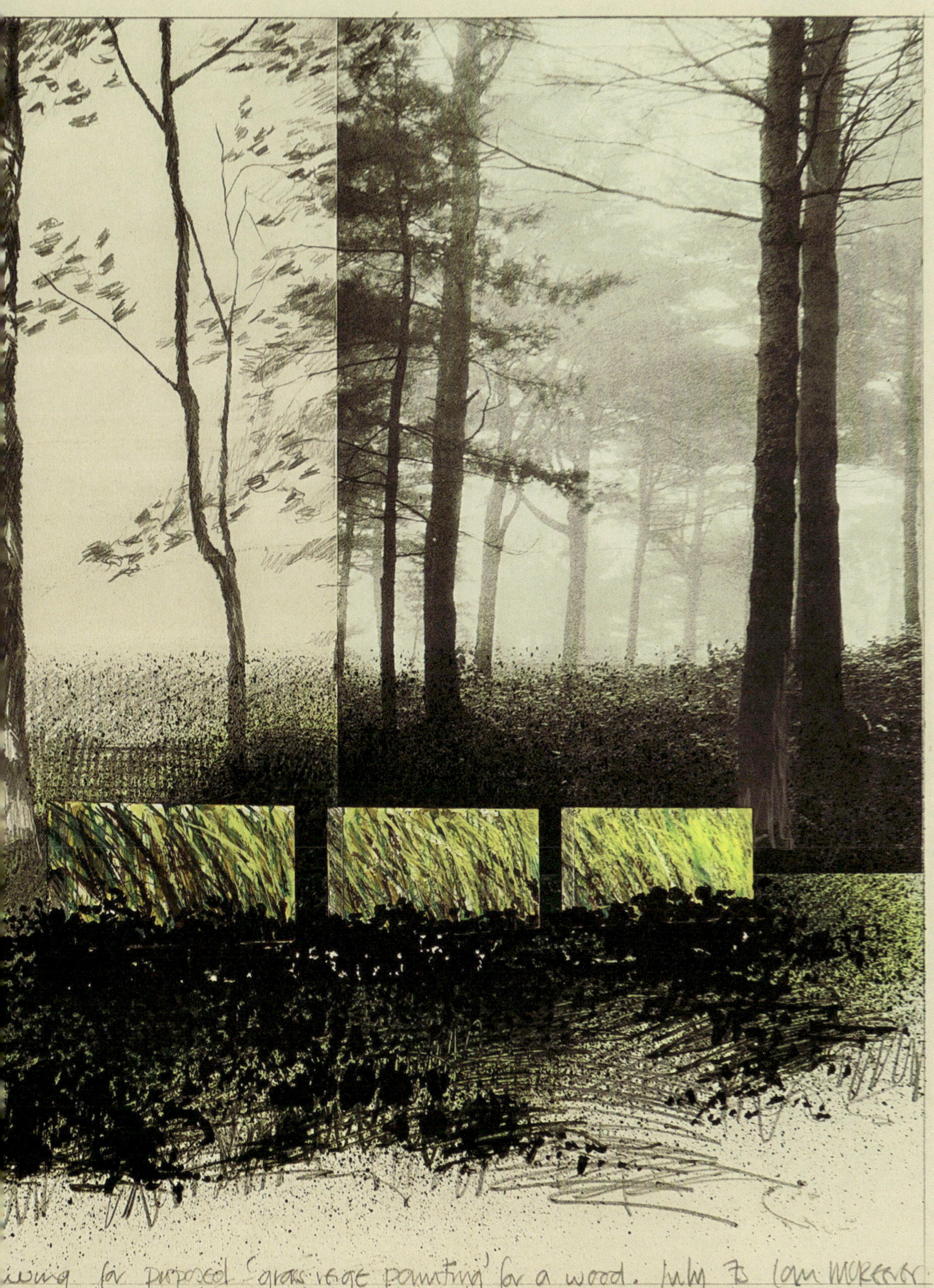

...wing for proposed 'grass verge painting' for a wood. July 75 Ian McKeever

It seems consequential that this transition occurred when it did. The end of the 1980s was a watershed in British art. The first half of the decade was notable for the reemergence of painting, both figurative and abstract, following its sidelining in the 1970s. British artistic culture had succumbed to pluralism. The empirical figuration of the painters known as 'The School of London' and the colourist abstraction of Howard Hodgkin and Gillian Ayres simultaneously attained international visibility. Painting's reclaiming of the British artistic agenda corresponded to the emergence, in the USA and Germany, of the brash, gestural painting of Julian Schnabel and Francesco Clemente, Sigmar Polke's virtuoso conflations of pop-cultural quotes, and Gerhard Richter's positing of a painter's oeuvre as a spectrum of disparate but coexisting idioms. Concurrently, a flourishing of British sculpture, through the work of artists such as Tony Cragg and Richard Deacon, blended a range of sculptural idioms, previously considered incompatible. Found objects were combined with the fabricated elements of traditional figurative sculpture. Formalist and minimalist modes were combined.

Common to these various developments was the reassertion of art's objecthood against its dematerialisation by 1970s conceptualism. The remaining threads of modernism's didactic cultural orthodoxy were stemmed. This was welcomed by some as a relief from the puritanism and parsimony of the art of the 1960s and 70s, as it was held by others to be critically dubious if not brazenly mercenary: a cynical regression into forms which had been definitively superseded.

In Britain, the recrudescence of traditional forms concealed underlying continuities, as had the rejection of those forms a decade previously. Perhaps the most influential British painters of the 1980s had been at work since the 1950s, if not earlier, and were only now acquiring greater recognition. Francis Bacon, Lucian Freud, Frank Auerbach, and Leon

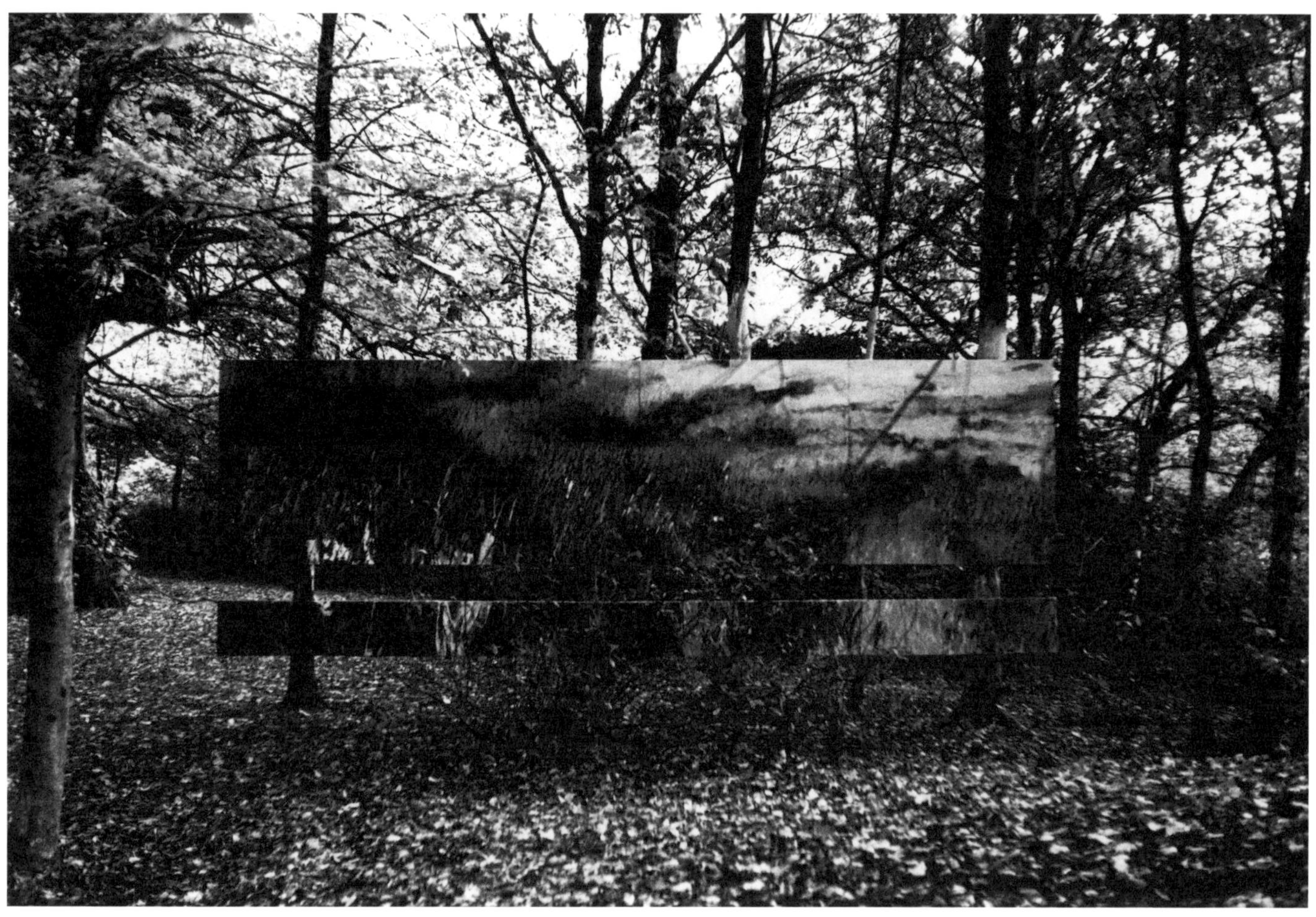

Kossoff produced paintings representing their primary experience of local subject matter: their families, close friends, and the London cityscape. Despite the apparent incongruence of figurative painting and conceptual art, the empirical, *a posteriori* philosophies of these painters corresponded to the defining characteristics of early British conceptual art which distinguished it from the conceptualism being practised in the USA or Germany. The Americans Robert Smithson and Walter de Maria were using landscape as both art site and art material, but were relatively unconcerned with how landscape might be represented; and if Joseph Kosuth was addressing representation itself it was on the terms of an abstract, linguisitic/visual relativism. In Germany, Franz Erhard Walther photographed his first and second 'Work Sets' (1963–76) in the empty fields of the Hochrhön region which surrounded his native city of Fulda. Although this landscape forms a dramatic backdrop in documentary photographs of performers 'using' Walther's canvas and plywood sculptures, it is not an element that is integral to the art but an expedient foil, sparse and expansive enough to allow the abstract geometries around which the sculptures were designed to be articulated as clearly as possible.

Early British conceptual art, however, is characterised by a concern with representation, and, more specifically, with the representation of landscape, that traditional repository of British artistic yearning. Richard Long may have adopted new, conceptual forms, such as photography and text, but they were used as a means of representing the British landscape. Susan Hiller is American, but her early art developed within the British conceptual context in which she found herself when she moved to London in the early 1970s. Her *Dedicated to the Unknown Artists* (1972–76) collates data from a collection of British picture postcards illustrating coastlines bombarded by stormy seas, their image placed in

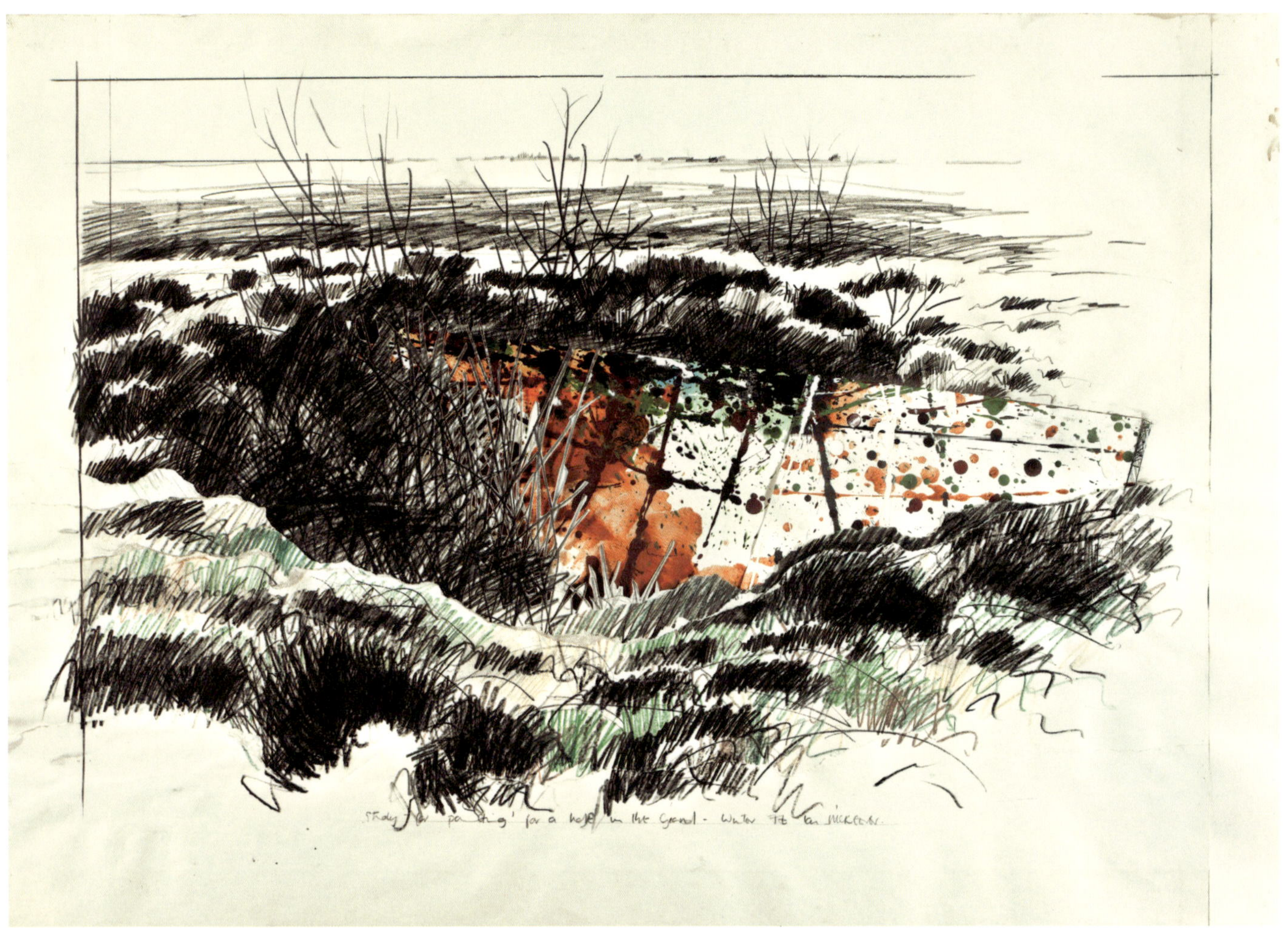

conjunction with diverse categories of typewritten, statistical analysis. Conceptual objectivity was brought to bear on landscape representation.

Born in 1946, in Withernsea, East Yorkshire, on the North Sea coast, Ian McKeever would have been familiar with such wave-terrorised shorelines, and early conceptualism of the British, landscape-oriented sort formed the artistic context in which he found himself when he moved to London in the early 1970s, a self-taught artist occupying one of the first Space studio sites at St. Katherine's Dock. In the two decades between that initial move to the capital and the end of the 1980s McKeever pursued an artistic dialogue between British conceptual methodology – predicated on landscape representation, but not painting – and large-scale abstract painting, influenced by the American modernist painting of the 1940s, 50s and 60s. These influences would have seemed incompatible, even paradoxical, at the time, but they reflected

twin poles within the British artistic culture of the period, an opposition which was only resolved by being superseded at the end of the 1980s by the international recognition of the art of Damien Hirst, Sarah Lucas and their contemporaries, whose constellations of pop-cultural signifiers, in the form of found-object-based sculptural assemblage, made distinctions between conceptualism and abstract painting seem immaterial. This was also when McKeever abandoned a dialectic between conceptualism and abstraction, and between photography and painting, and progressed into a practice of painting-in-itself. It was also when, having lived and worked in central London since the beginning of the 1970s, he and his family resettled in the farmhouse in rural Dorset in which they still live.

From Richard Long's itemised treks through the British countryside, to Susan Hiller's collating of circumstantial

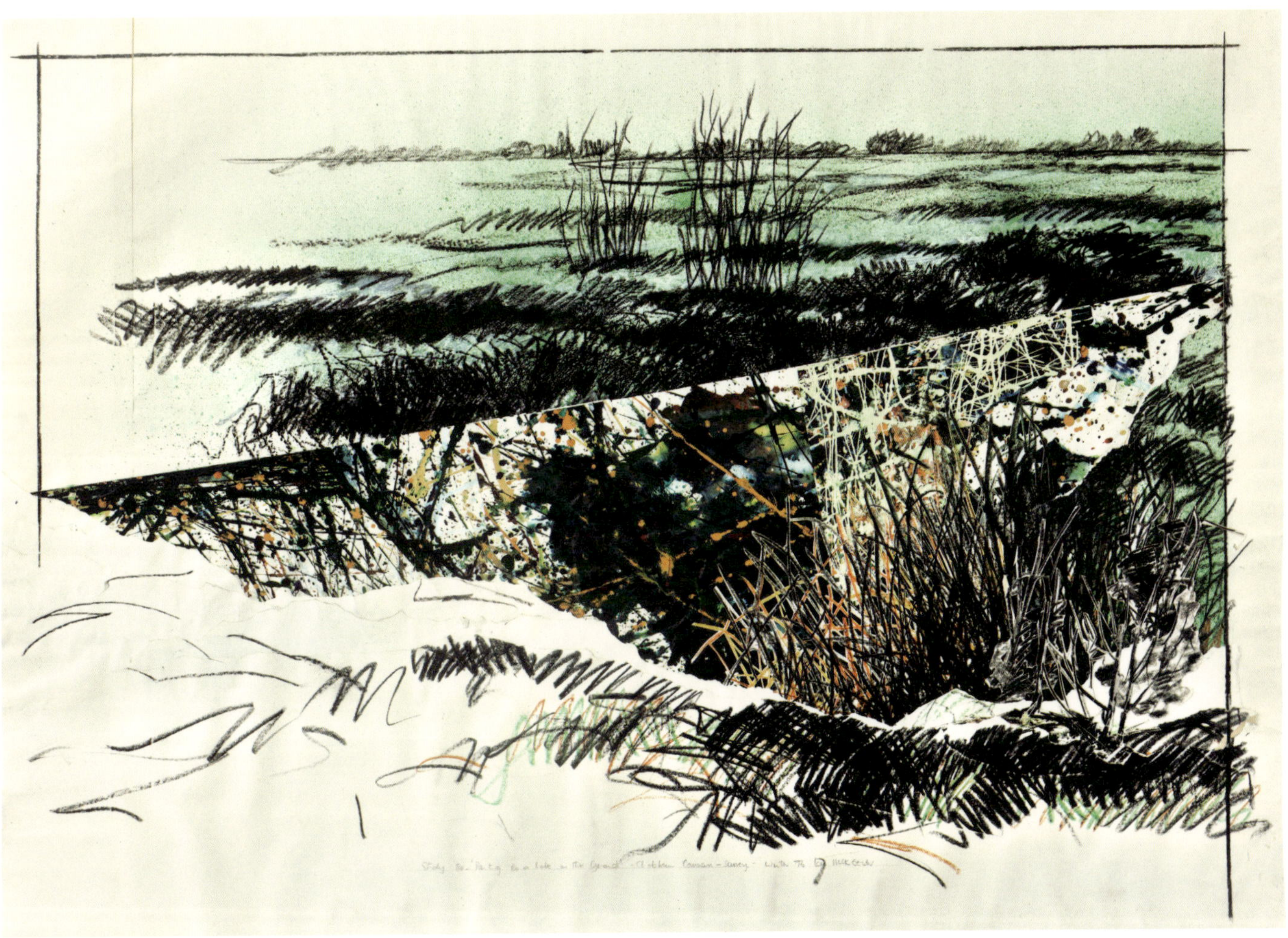

data from vintage postcards, to the Boyle Family's fibreglass reconstructions of random sections of the earth's surface, early British conceptual art sought new means to achieve many of the representational ends to which painting and drawing had strived throughout the British artistic tradition, while holding the structures of representation itself up to scrutiny. McKeever's earliest work both conforms to this context and is exceptional within it. He applied its methods to painting, the medium which the work of his conceptual-orientated peers defined itself by rejecting. Susan Hiller, for example, cut up her old canvases into small squares, and compacted them into frayed cubes of tinted fabric, printed with a date consigning them to the period the paintings had been made ('Painting Blocks', 1970–84). The traditional processes had become archival fodder.

McKeever conformed to this context by treating painting as a questionable medium which could only be adopted once it had been subjected to critical deconstruction. His earliest landscape-based projects, realised between 1972 and 1976, present the medium as an artificial screen that polarises itself against or is assimilated by the landscape into which it was placed. The paintings he produced for these projects were not intended to be aesthetically discrete, autonomous works, but signs of their own activity, impersonally executed to avoid signature marks that would detract from their role as elements within a broader dialectic. The paintings signified the qualities which would define them as painting in contrast to the natural activity against which they were to be pitted.

For *Painting for a Hole in the Ground* (1976–77), the last of these outdoor projects, McKeever produced a large, abstract painting in his London studio and transported it to Chobham Common in Surrey – an area of open, unstructured landscape – where it was left in a ditch from October to January of the following year. During those three months the elements

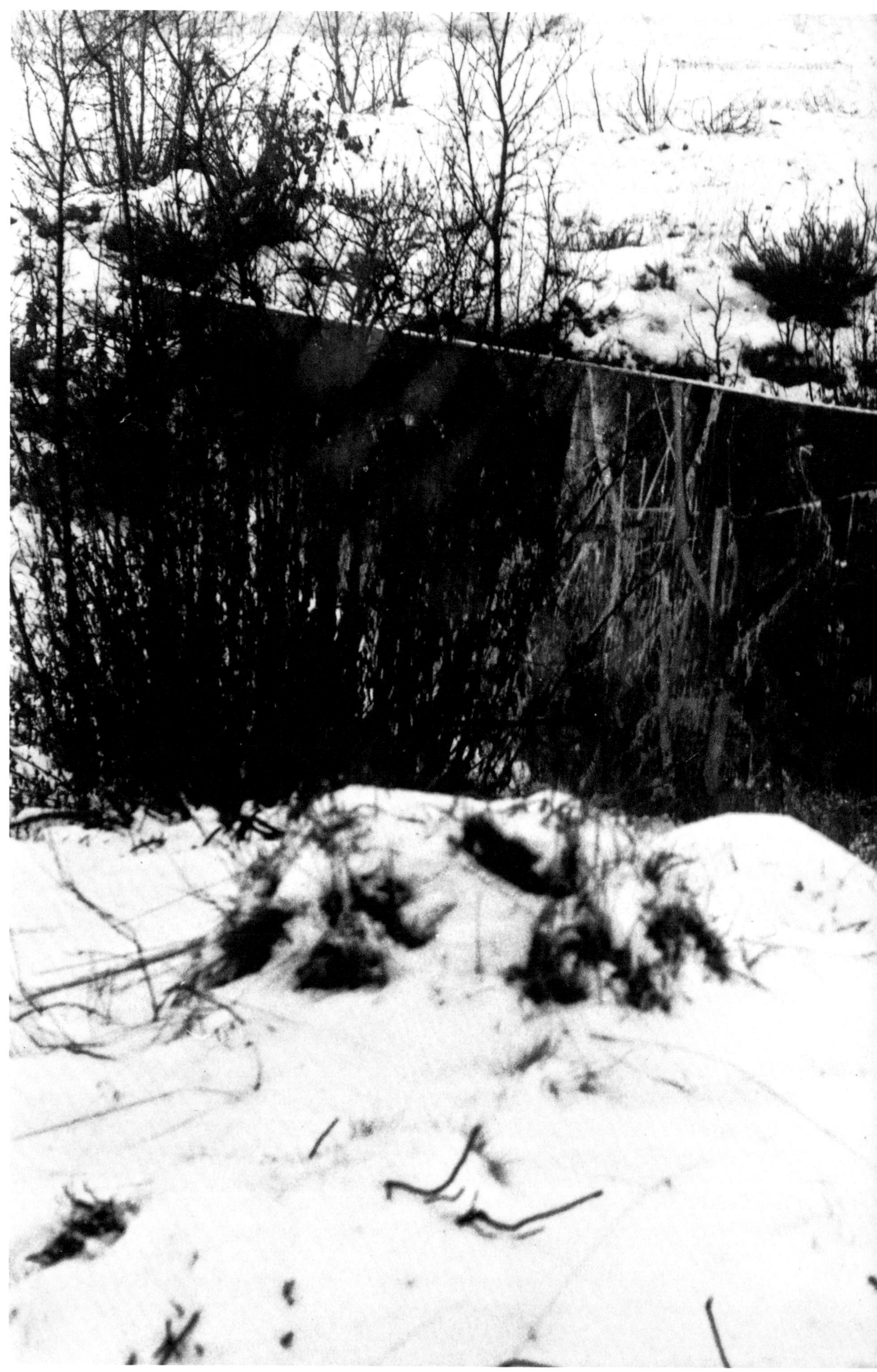

*Painting for a Hole in
the Ground, Chobham
Common, Surrey,
1976–1977*

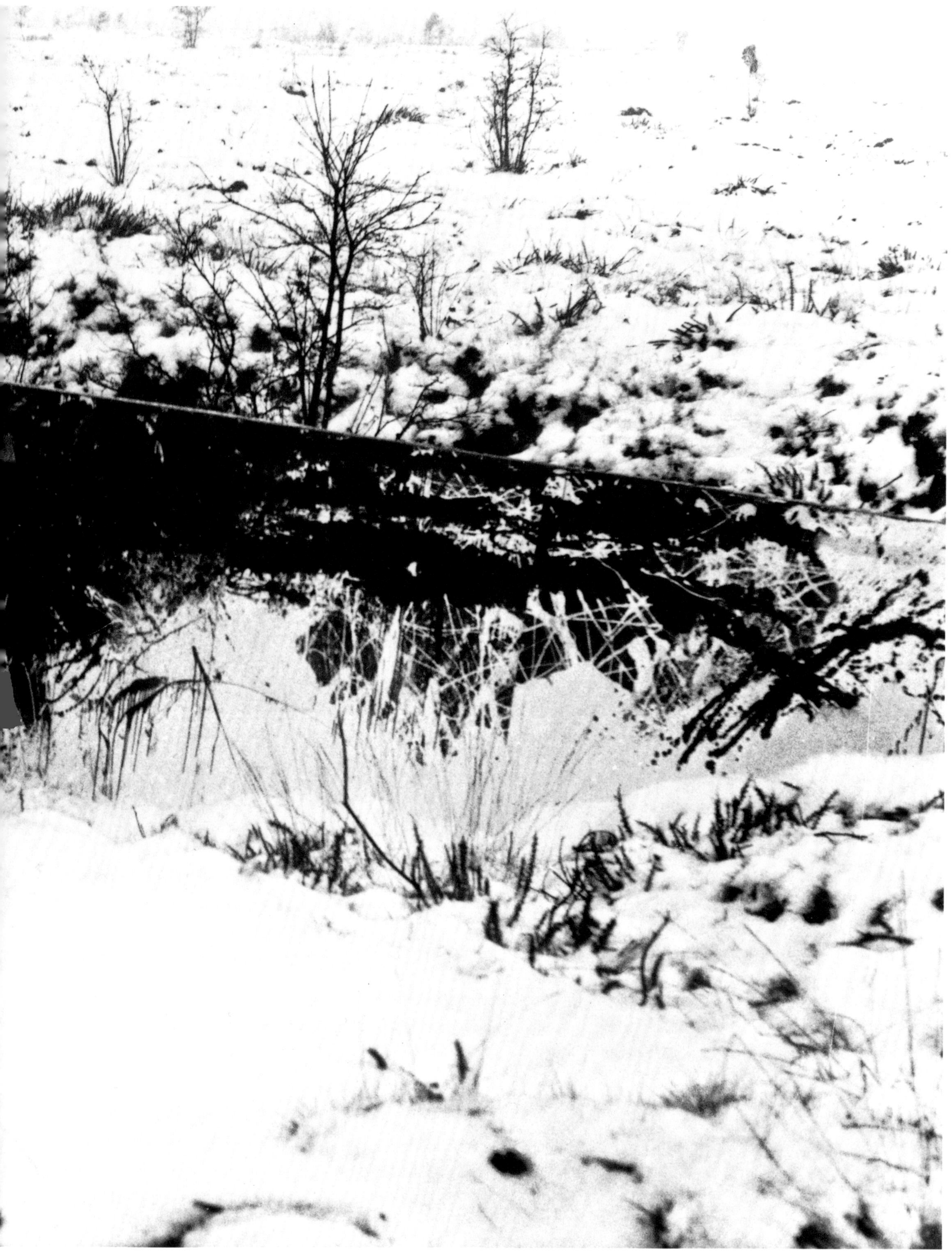

worked on the canvas where McKeever had left off. The painting was several metres wide and executed in an Abstract Expressionist idiom. Its streaks and splashes of paint reproduce with the highest possible contrast in the black-and-white photographs which were all that was left of the project after the painting had been removed from its site and destroyed. Jutting out of a declavity in the earth the painting seems tailored to the wide rectangle of the photograph's 35mm frame, as the spray of branches and tufts of long grass along the lip of the ditch merge seamlessly into the painterly incident behind them. It is as though McKeever's testing of the interface between culture and nature had been most incisively enacted within the photograph itself, although it is only a documentary record and not the art itself. By fusing two sides of McKeever's dialectic – landscape and painting – under the auspices of the photograph that represents them both, the images symbolically perform the final fusion towards which the entire project was tending. By outlasting them both, the photograph reconciles the two sides of McKeever's equation.

The ultimate primacy of a photographic record over the work of art it records was not lost on McKeever, nor was it a unique perception to have arisen in the context of early conceptual art's deployment of photography to document ephemeral or performative works. John Hilliard's photography developed out of a recognition that what was left of his early sculptural installations, all subsequently destroyed, was their photographic documentation. In the USA, a corresponding perception led Lawrence Weiner to abandon his early, performative actions for the short texts which were written as instructions for their performance when he realised that the texts stood for and ultimately replaced both action and object, becoming the art they were intended to prompt. For McKeever, photography had emerged as a third, overseeing element in a triad of painting/landscape/photograph, and one which would shortly replace the landscape as one of the two primary dialectical elements, while landscape was relegated to the motif towards which each generates its own relative response.

Whereas McKeever's ephemeral landscape projects conformed to one aspect of early British conceptual methodology – performative, time-based, exploratively empirical, and resistant to being confined to the form of the durable art object – his 'Sand and Sea' series, produced concurrently, is monochrome, gridded, data-rich, conforming to an emphasis on objective research associated with early conceptual art objects that were intended to last. At the centre of *Series No.5*, (Withernsea, East Yorkshire, Spring 1977), is a figurative drawing of a beach, curving in towards the sea. The functionality and impersonality of the drawing's figuration corresponds to the generic, gestural abstraction of the painting McKeever produced for *Painting for a Hole in the Ground*. Both efficiently foreground a type of information which should be legible enough to highlight a contrast with other types of information: in *Painting for a Hole in the Ground*, with the natural growth of the landscape itself as an alternative 'language'; in *Sand and Sea Series No.5*, with a series of fifteen smaller, collaged vignettes, representing the activity of sea water, which frame the central image, their spectrum functioning as a relativistic rebuttal of the single representation they surround.

The contrast lies not merely in the distinction between the traditional, perspectival illusionism of the central image and the relatively shallow, pictorial space of the surrounding vignettes. Each of the smaller images is composed of two media collaged together, their juncture imitating the uneven line of surf encroaching on sand. A photograph of water abuts a drawing of sand; or a form of trompe l'oeil illusionism enters the conceit when a drawing is placed onto the beach and

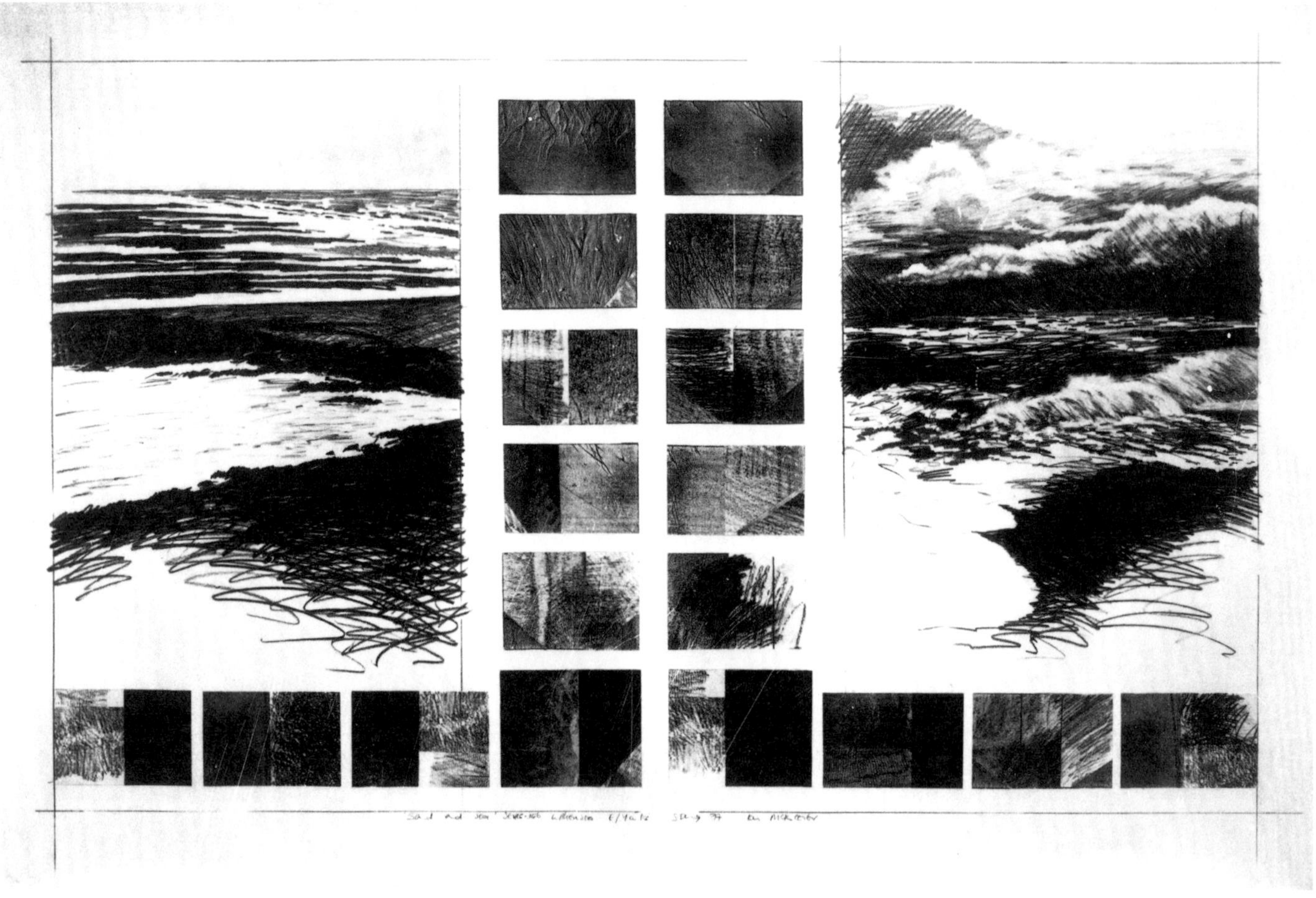

photographed as it is submerged by the water it represents. That photograph is then cut into the curved shape of the surf's edge and collaged over a photograph or drawing of sand. Each of these vignettes questions the representational assumptions on which the central drawing is based. The recognisable outline of surf creeping over sand seduces the viewer into a sense of recognition to which the details of the image, on closer scrutiny, refuse to confirm. The gridded format suggests an accretion of heterogeneous data that conforms to a familiar early conceptual art template, but in order to challenge the foundations of that template in a cognitive model of rationally orderable perception.

McKeever's blurring of conventional distinctions between photography and drawing entrains phenomenological ambiguities. A representation of a subject proves to be a representation of the subject's representation. A photographic image halting time proves to be a drawn image composed in time.

What appears to be an image of a familiar, natural phenomenon is a deconstruction of the workings of representation itself: a series of shuffling screens never revealing the subject they all claim to address. It is typical of McKeever's instinct for dynamic oppositions that the subject he adopted as a pretext for this analytical process, should have been one of personal significance to him: his childhood home. He chose a location loaded with subjective, emotive associations to render inaccessible through a structuralistic process. The act of distancing is therefore charged by the closeness of the motif.

This give-and-take between proximity to a subject and the objectivity which ratifies and rationalises it would become crucial to McKeever's approach. Like *Painting for a Hole in the Ground* and McKeever's other, site-specific, landscape-based works, the 'Sand and Sea' series posits drawing and photography as correlatives of this dichotomy, but unstably and interchangeably so. Drawing is physically immediate and

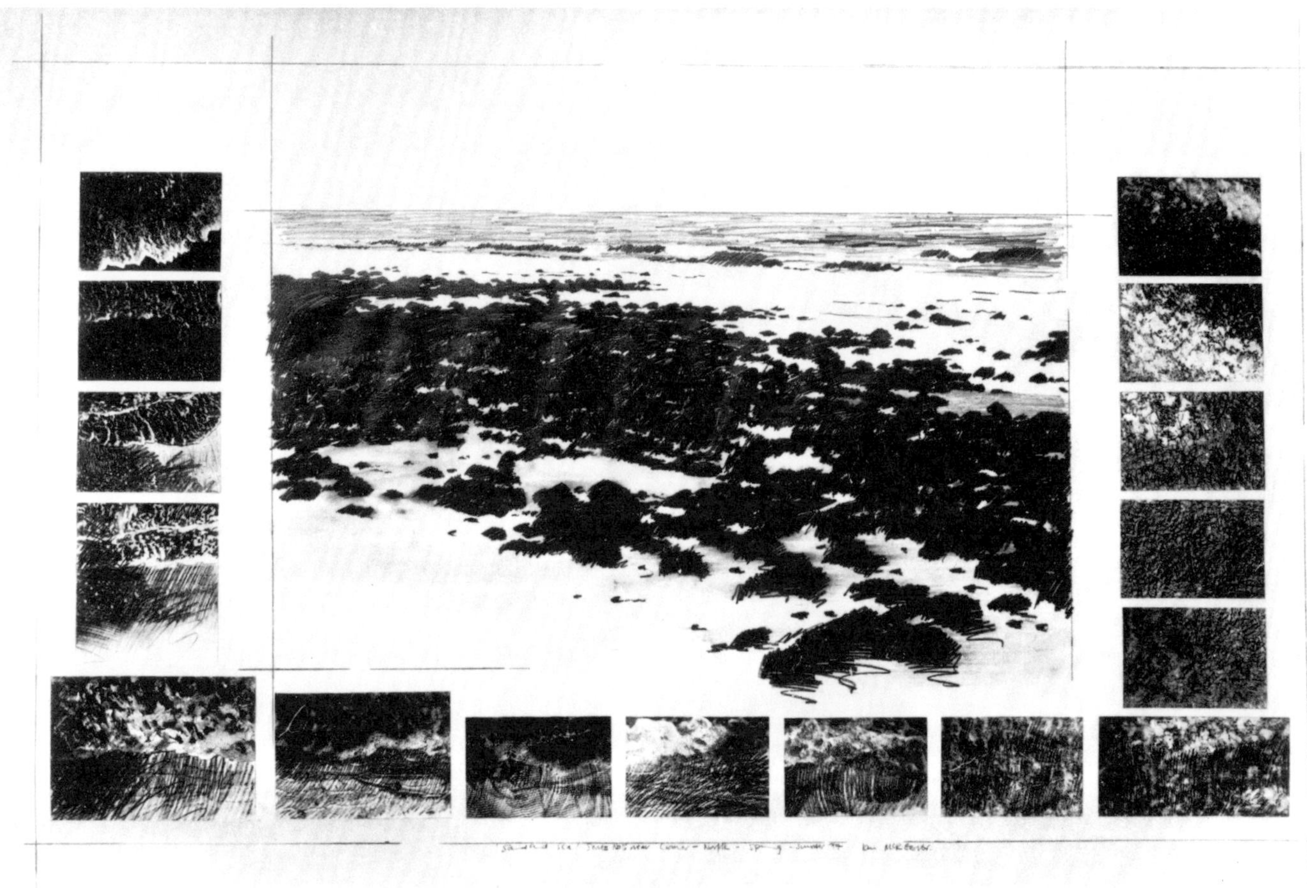

leaves a causal trace of the artist's touch. There is a sense in which no artistic medium could be closer to the artist. But the contrary is also true: a photograph provides causal access, not to the artist's hand, but through light's exposure of the film to the subject of the image itself, allowing it a greater power to authenticate its referent. In this sense it is closer to its subject. The instantaneity with which a photographic image is exposed gives it a perceptual immediacy which contrasts with the layering of perceptions out of which a drawing is composed.

The grey areas between photography and painting's respective grasps of their subjects defined McKeever's work of the following decade, as the series structure of 'Sand and Sea' series would become his preferred framing mechanism, placing parameters around an area of inquiry from which he could progress into another set of preoccupations newly designated to indicate the shift in emphasis. This early-conceptual method of framing the narrative of an artist's development tends to partition into discrete thematic blocks an aesthetic narrative, and a painterly one, which can also be interpreted, with greater hindsight, as a continuous evolution. In his transition from the 'Sand and Sea' series to the 'Field' series (1977–78), the most significantly altered factor is that of scale: from the horizontal, window-scale view of the former, to a human scale, full-frontal and vertical, emphasising an artwork's palpable physical presence. The shift enabled McKeever to test his conceptualism more directly upon the senses.

Over the next decade, the vertical rectangular canvas, approximately corresponding to the height of a standing viewer – an inheritance of scale from US Abstract Expressionism – would become McKeever's staple format. Conforming to the easel-scale of a traditional landscape painting, the 'Sand and Sea' series encourages the viewer to perceive its horizontal rectangle as a picture to peruse. The 'Field' series adds a

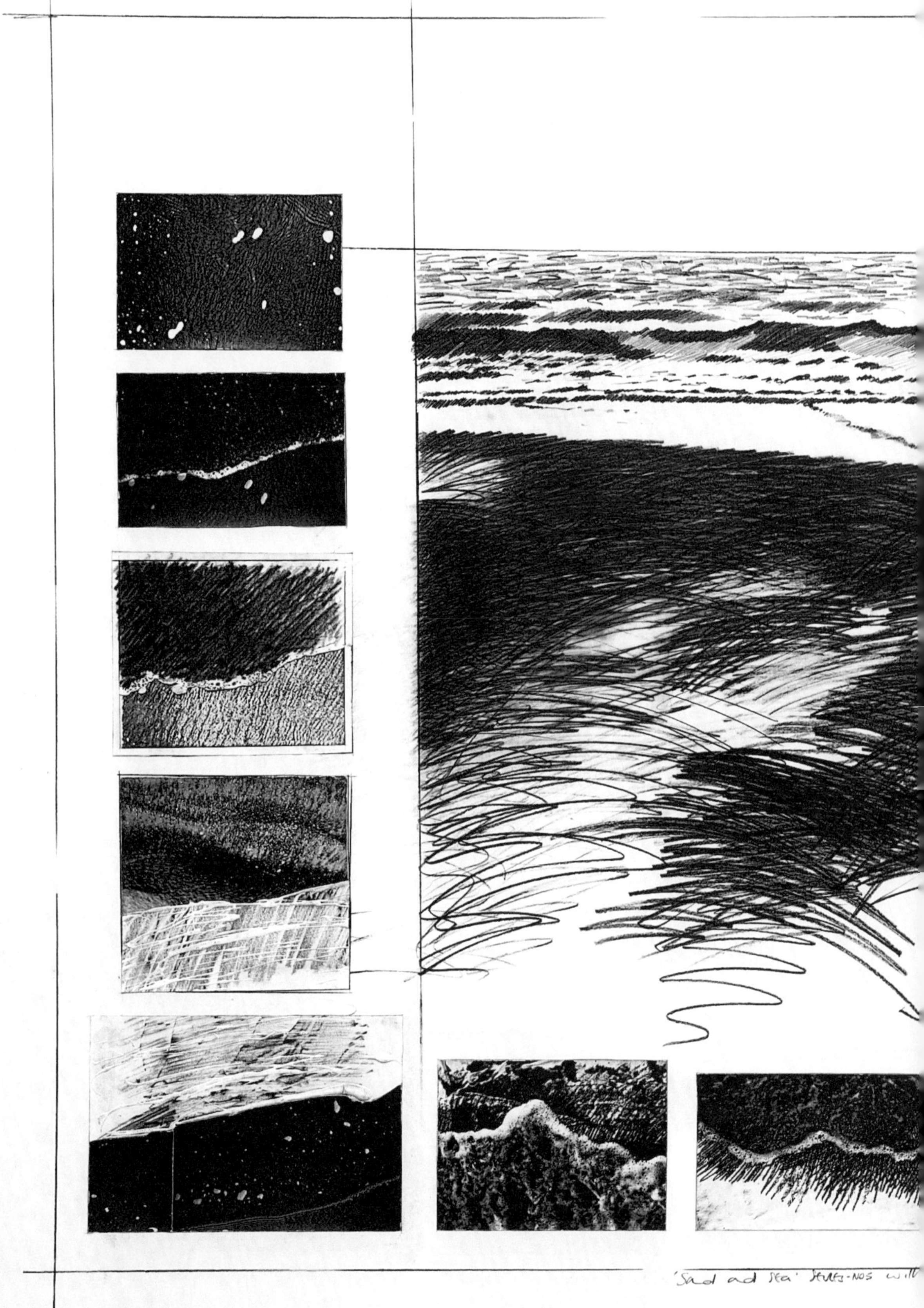
'Sand and Sea' Studies-Nos with

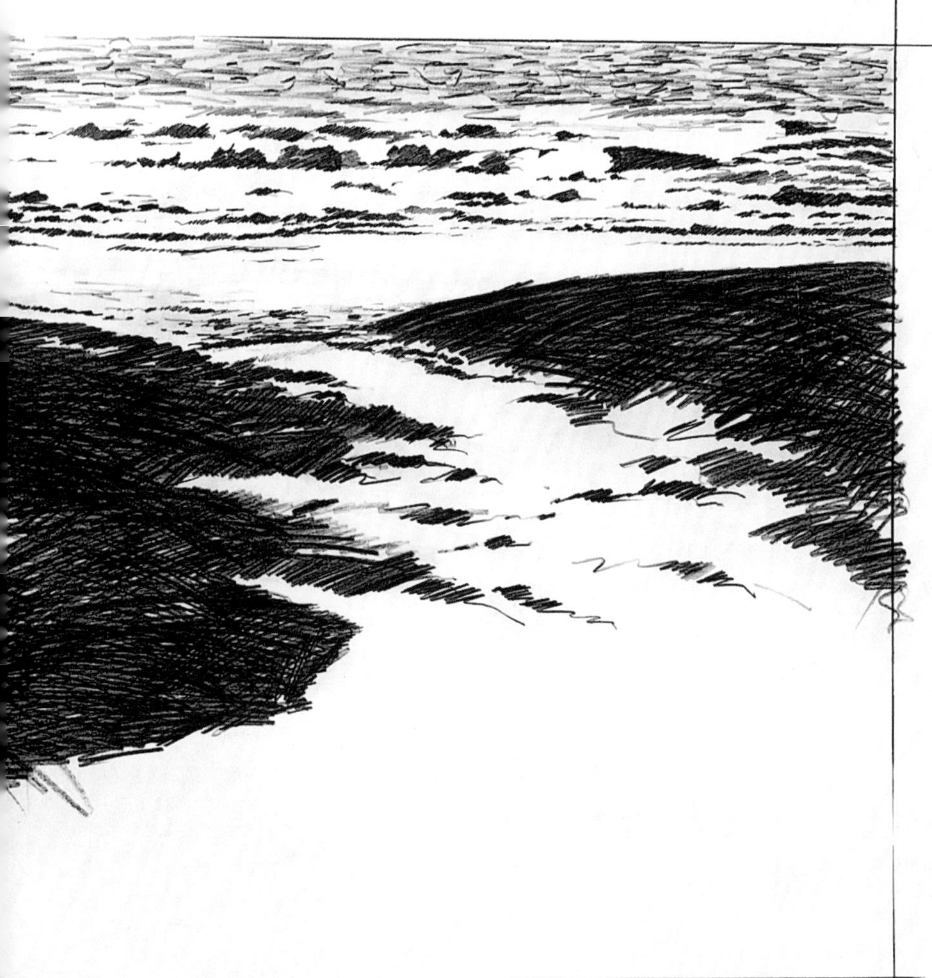
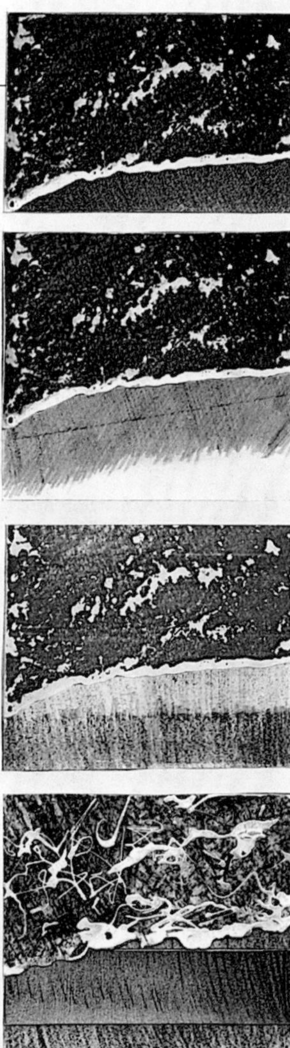
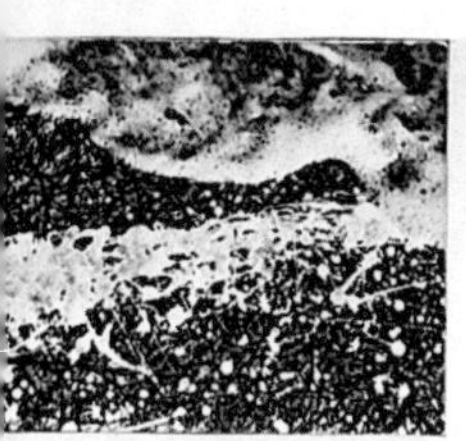
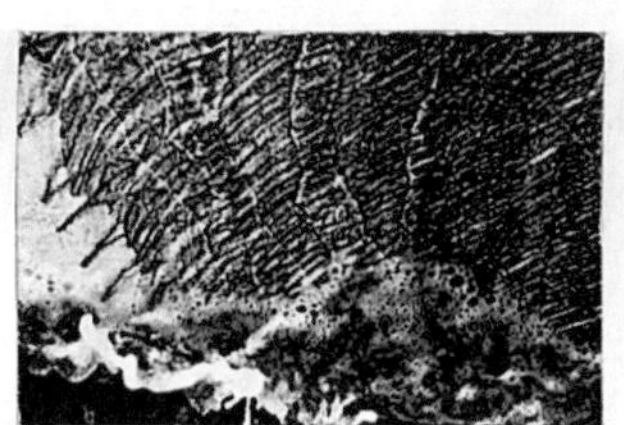
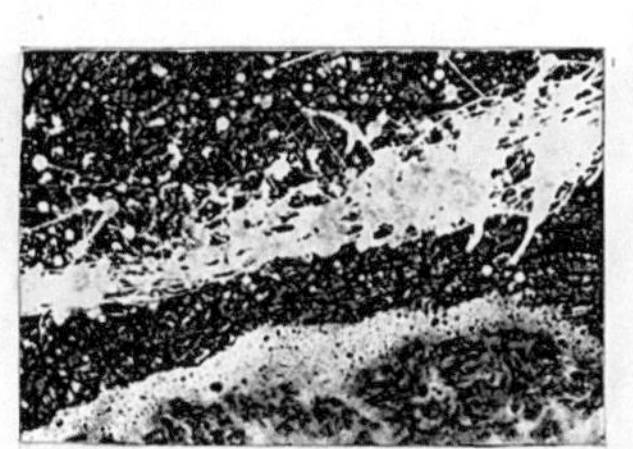
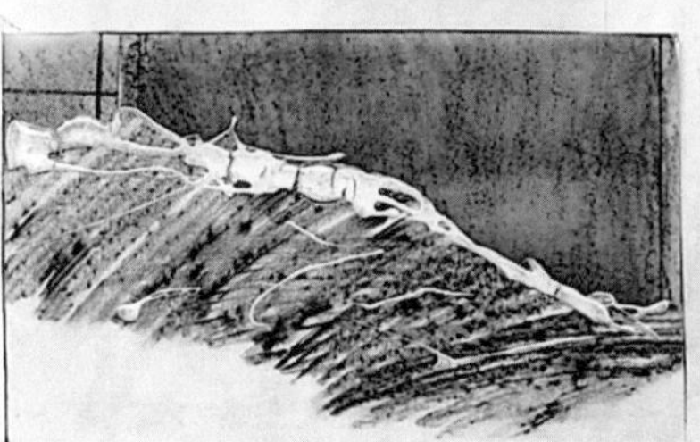

...ts_ Spring 74   Ian McKeever.

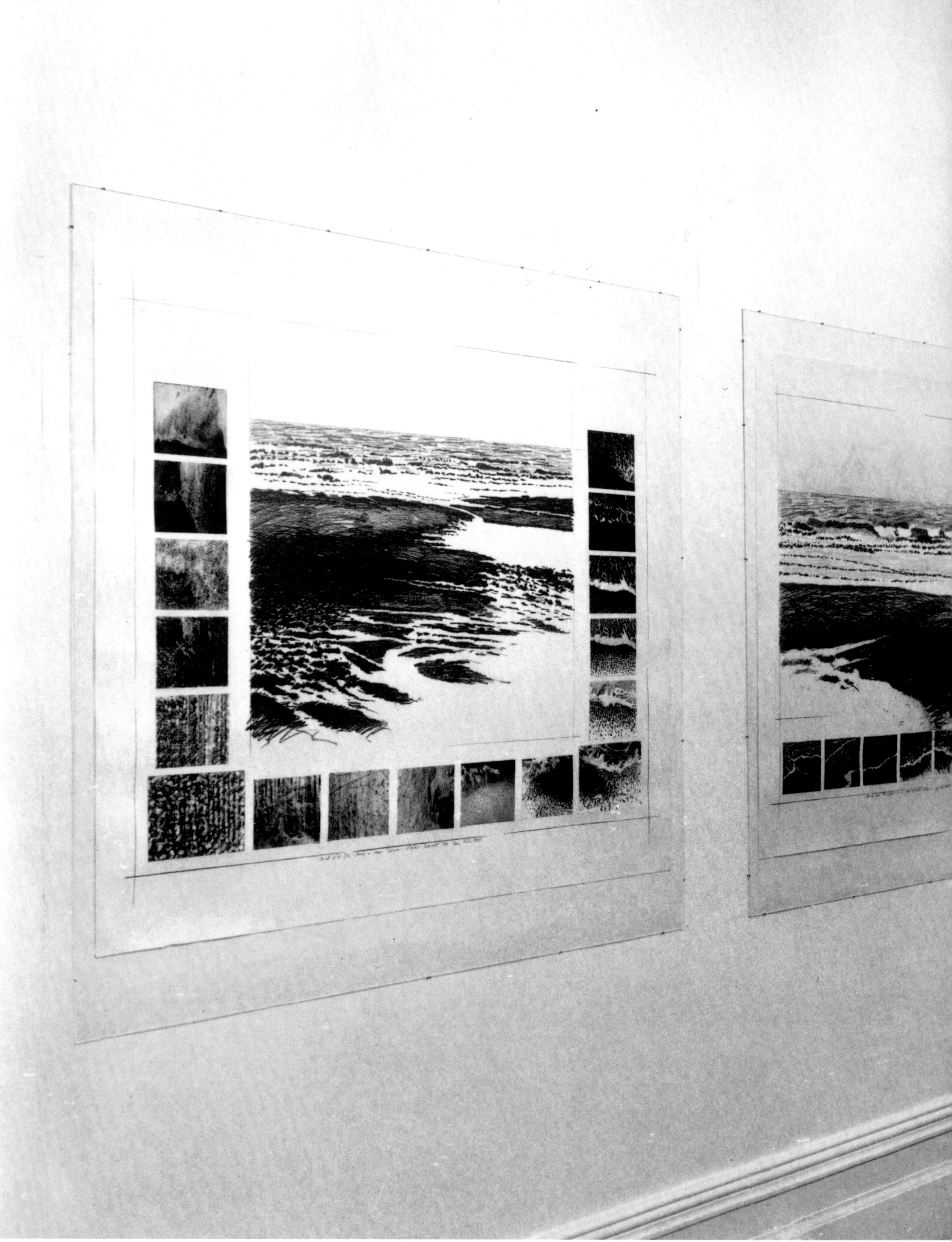

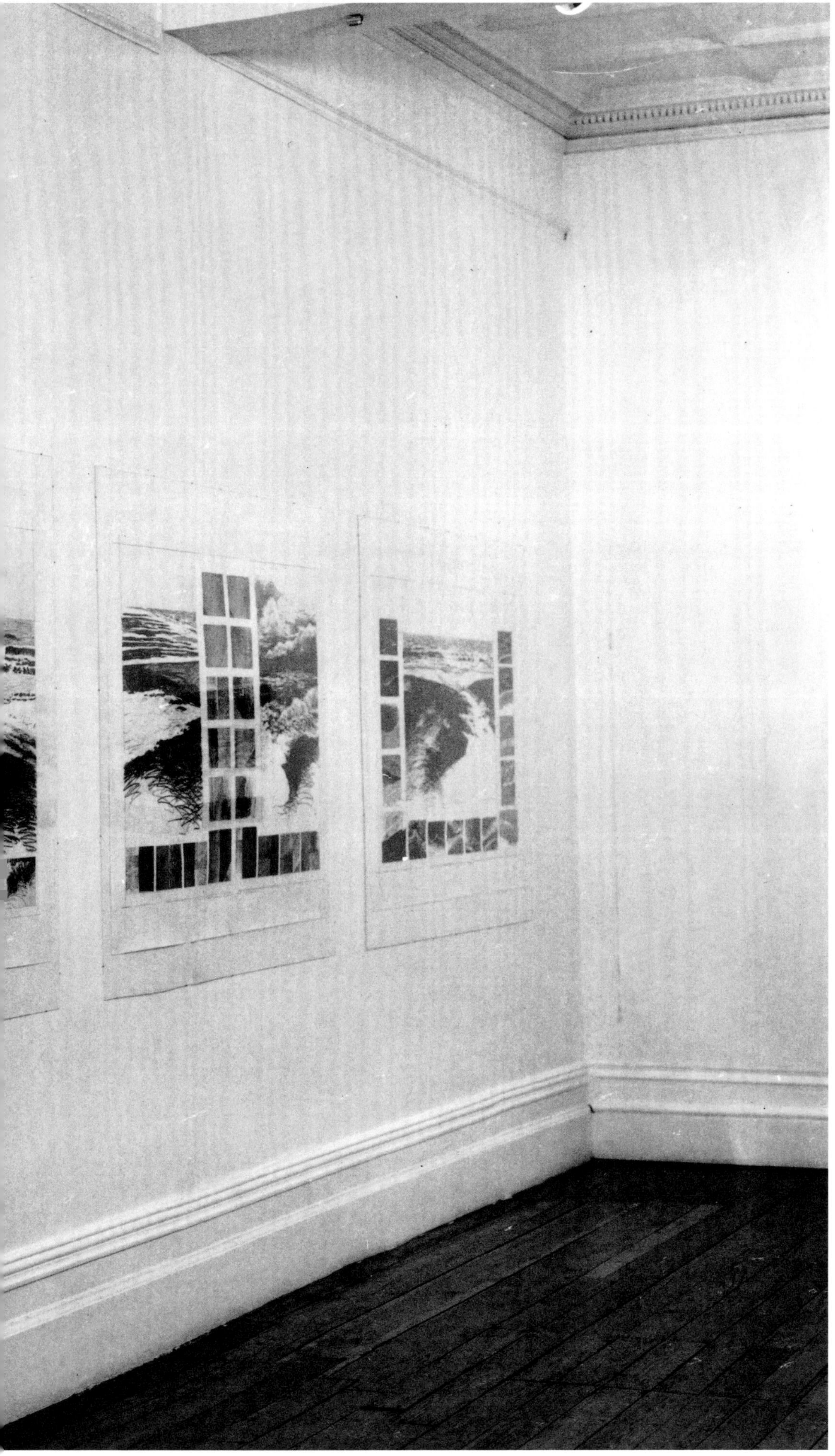

Sand and Sea Series,
Nigel Greenwood
Gallery, 1977

more physically active dimension to a viewer's perceptual engagement with the work. We confront the otherness and abstraction of a field of physically-applied mark-making before stepping back to test the extent to which the marks resolve into a pictorial portal. The word 'field' has multiple implications: a field within a landscape; a field of research; but also the field of the paper which is the work's ground and on which the strokes of a drawing or the aggregate of a photograph have left their marks.

The 'Field' series also marks McKeever's first use of the diptych format, bringing two separate but abutting pictorial elements into dialectical conjunction. Subsequently, he would use the format in its more traditional format, placing two constituent elements side-by-side. Here, however, a vertical drawing is positioned directly above a smaller, horizontal photograph of the same width, combining the two elements into a single, vertical rectangle of approximately figure-height. Unusually in landscape imagery, height corresponds to illusionistic depth. Each work features a drawn, horizontal line above which the paper is left bare. There is irony in McKeever's demonstration of the glibness of the perceptual reflex with which we automatically 'read' such a line as a horizon.

The style of the drawing below the line fluctuates in and out of representational legibility, confirming an illusion of a landscape's depth or contradicting it by treating the paper as an area to cover with automatic gestural markmaking, onlyto allow the line to claim these marks for the illusionisticdepth it summarily signifies. The line's power to invest a 'field' of drawing with illusionistic space is exploited even as the line is exposed as a mere geometric abstraction by the non-referential mark-making below it and by its echoing of the parallel division between the drawing and the photograph, each individually framed.

From the 1990s onwards, McKeever has increasingly attempted to neutralise the autobiographical aspect of painterly gesture, impersonalising the painted mark so as not to confine it to its causal link to a single maker. But his earliest work – such as the generic action painting of *Painting for a Hole in the Ground* or the automatic, gestural drawing of the 'Field' series – already held the self-proclamation of gestural painting at a critical arm's length. The mark-making of the 'Field' series is that of an artist objectifying his own process into that of a 'drawing machine' that might be equivalent to the camera's mechanical function.

The drawn horizon line of the 'Field' series is an early example of McKeever's dramatisation of the relation between empiricism and belief, especially as it pertains to a viewer's engagement with painting and photography. Perception of a painting shifts between consciousness of it as a material object, composed of paint applied to a flat surface, and as a pictorial plane giving onto illusionistic space. The former perception is objective and materialistic, while the latter requires a suspension of disbelief. The experience of looking at a photograph – even in the large-scale formats with which many contemporary artists emphasise the medium's objecthood – is relatively biased towards illusionism. Although this illusion demands a more unqualified suspension of disbelief, an analogue photograph asks of its viewer a lesser investment of belief than a painting because its evidential link to its referent seems relatively incontrovertible.

The 'Field' series challenges these assumptions. The drawn horizon line coerces our susceptibility to pictorial illusion as tendentiously as a photograph, although it is surrounded by abstract mark-making which refutes its claims. Similarly, the separate photographic element is made to exploit its position as an extension of the drawing's illusionistic space into a further

cont'd on p.34

Field Series, 1978
(12 individual works)

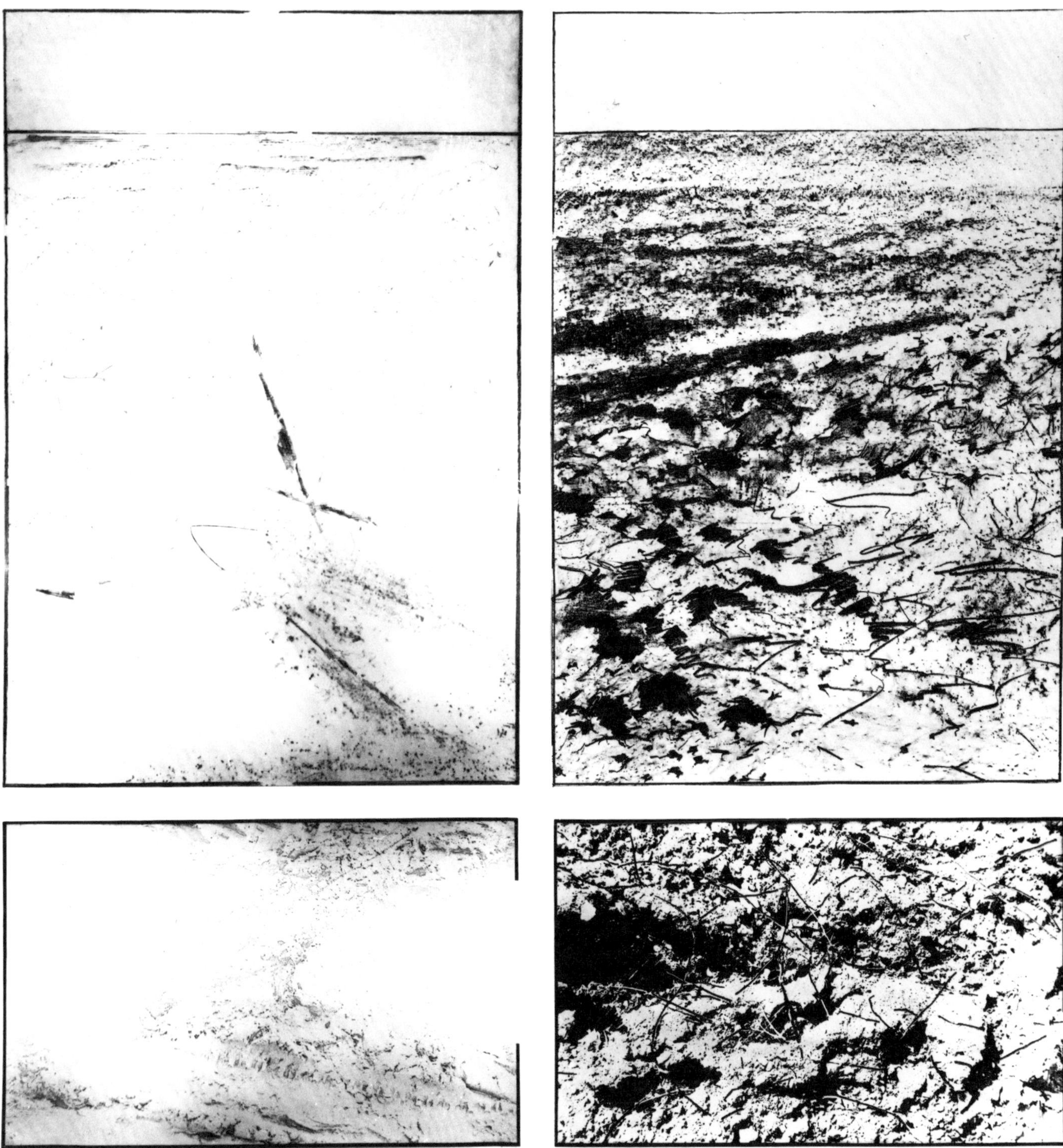

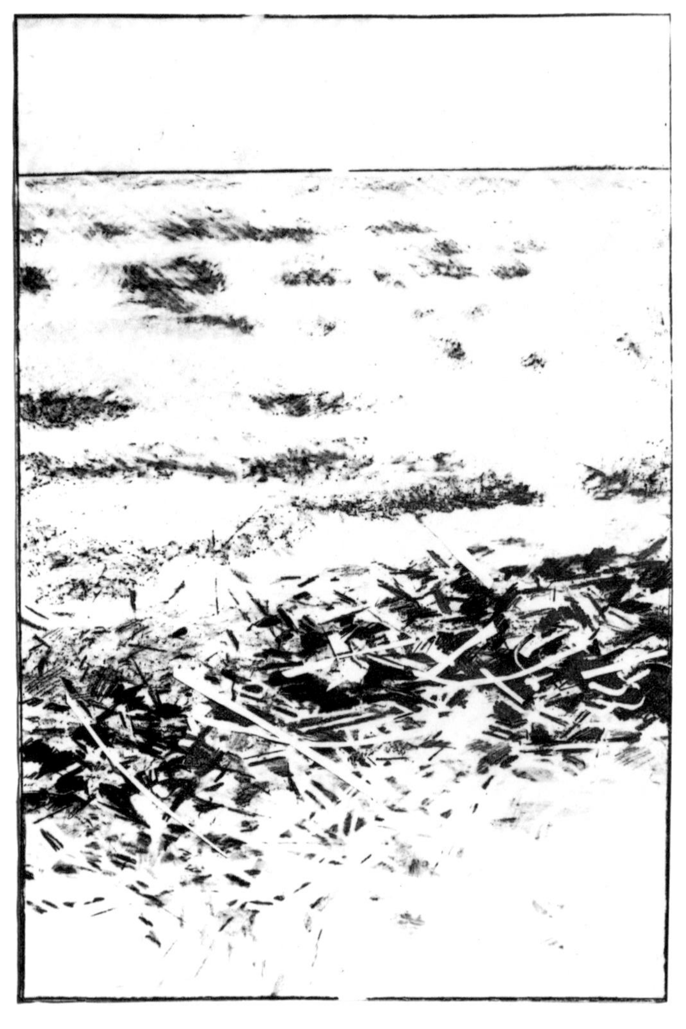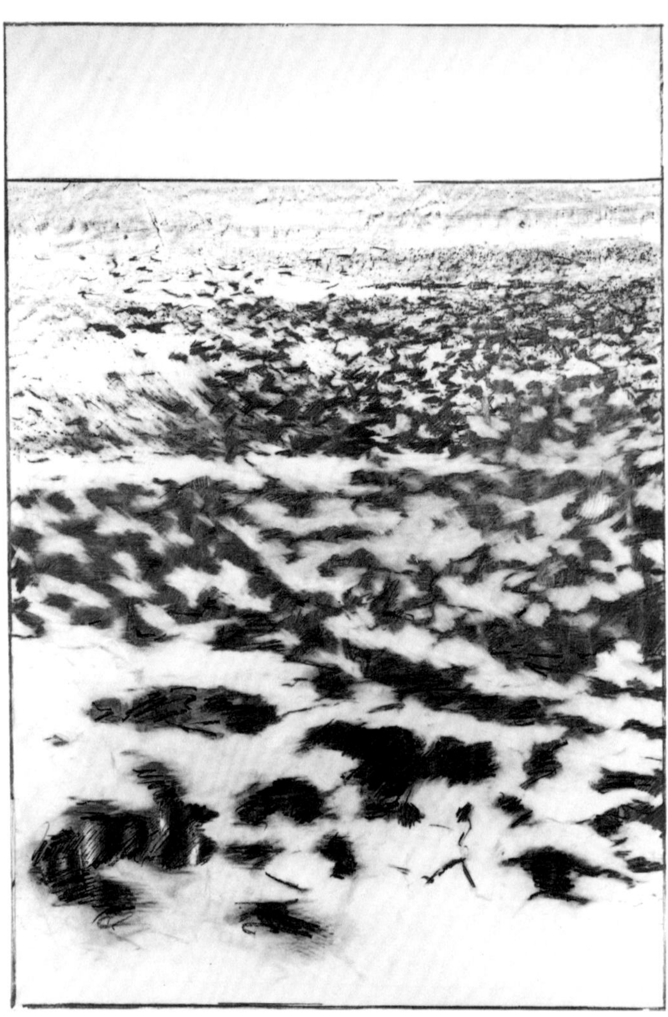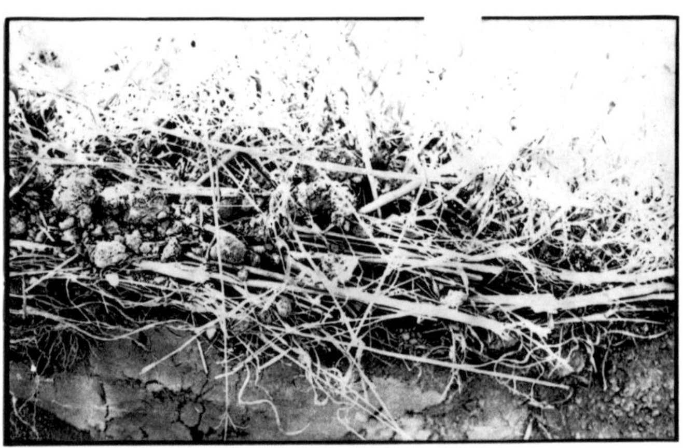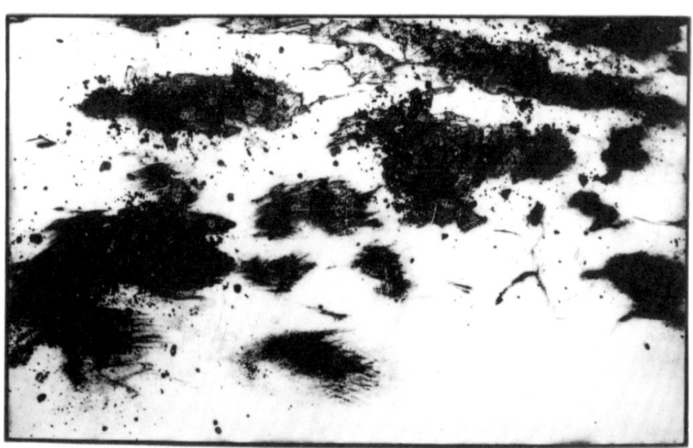

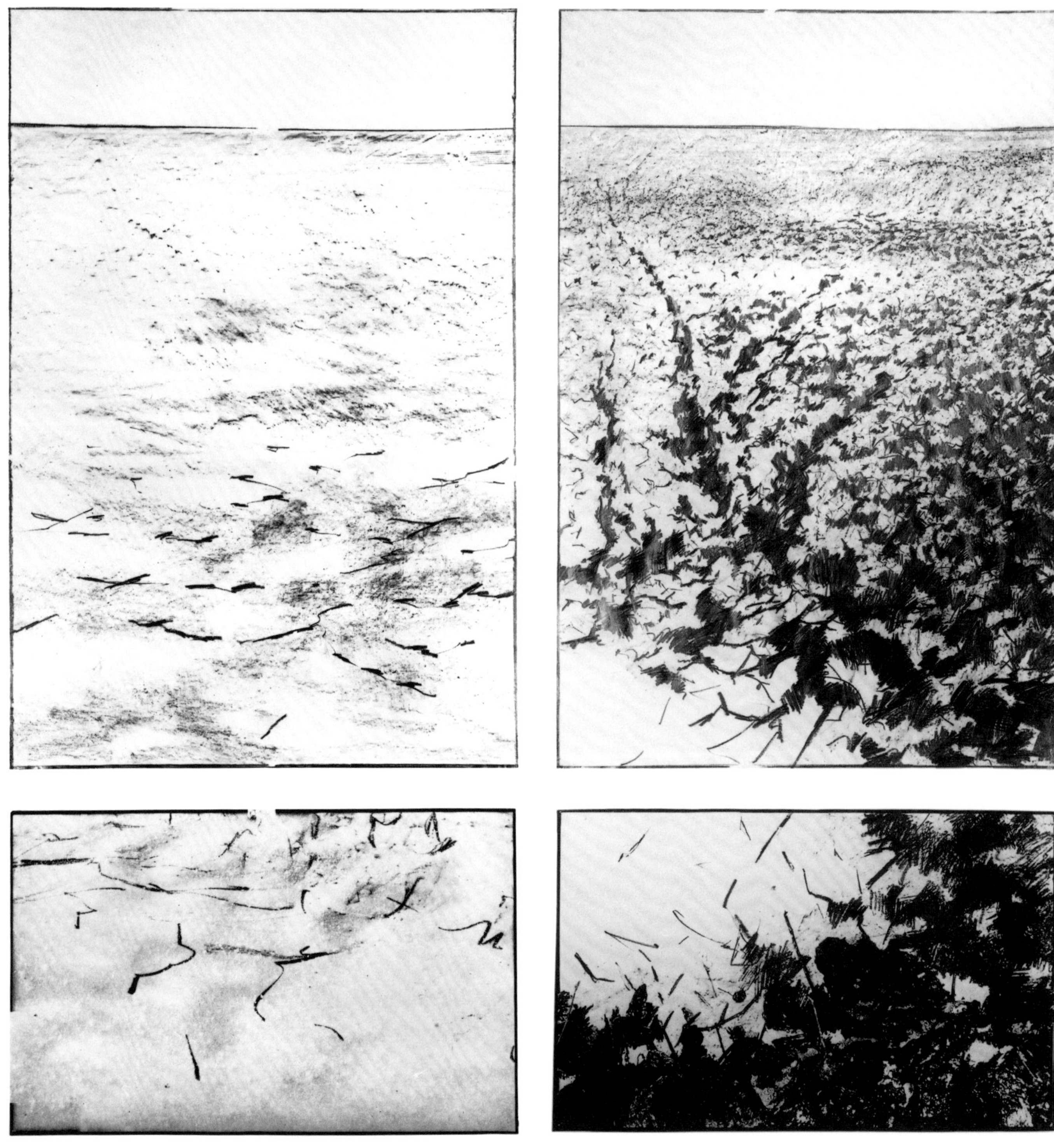

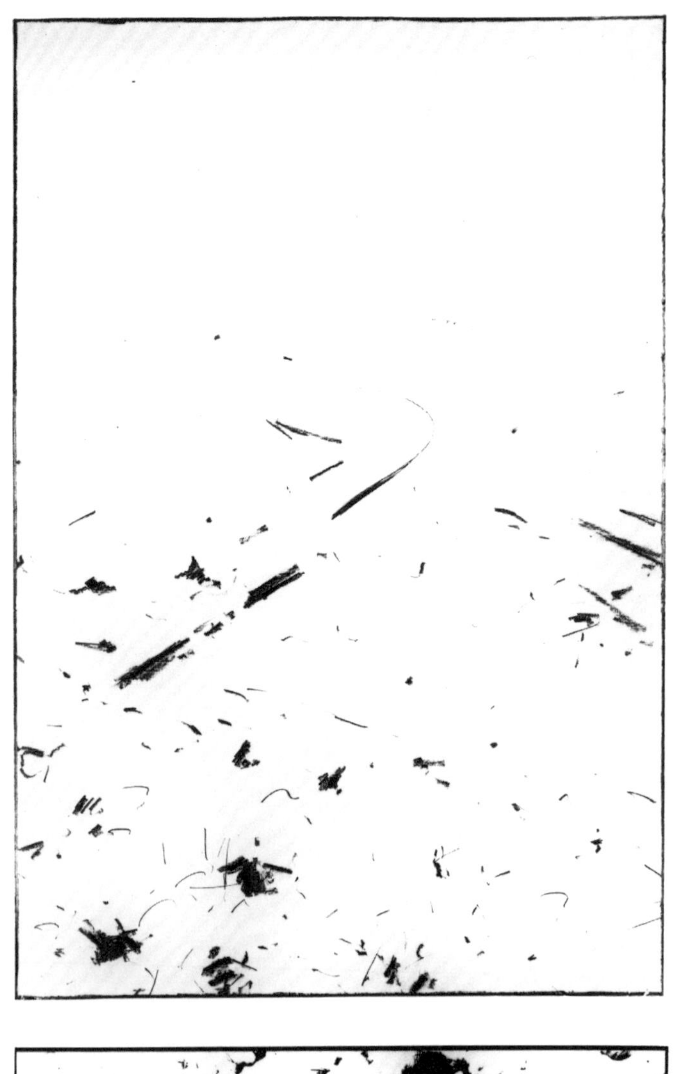

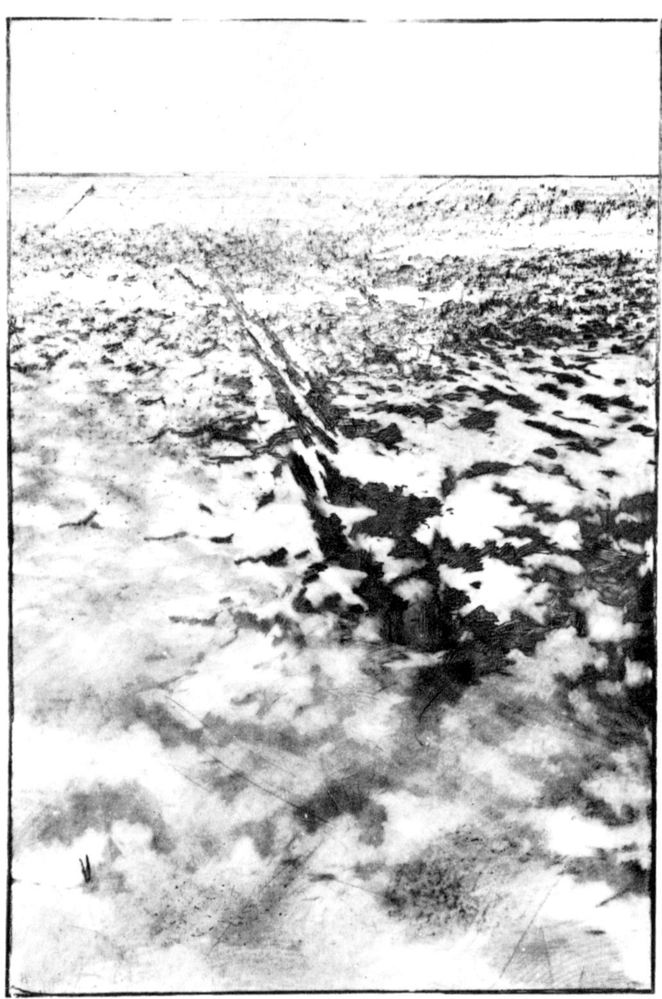

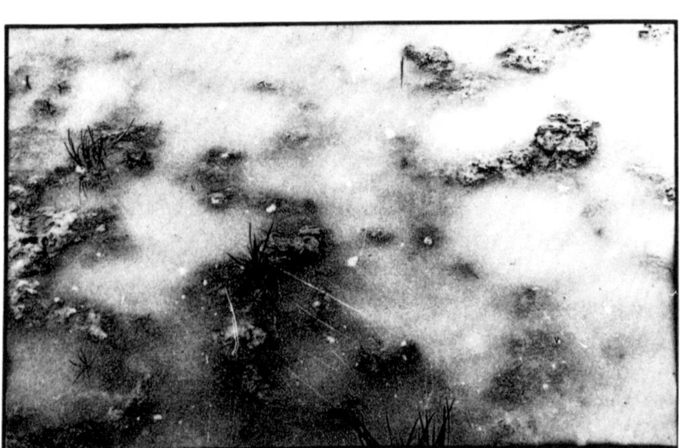

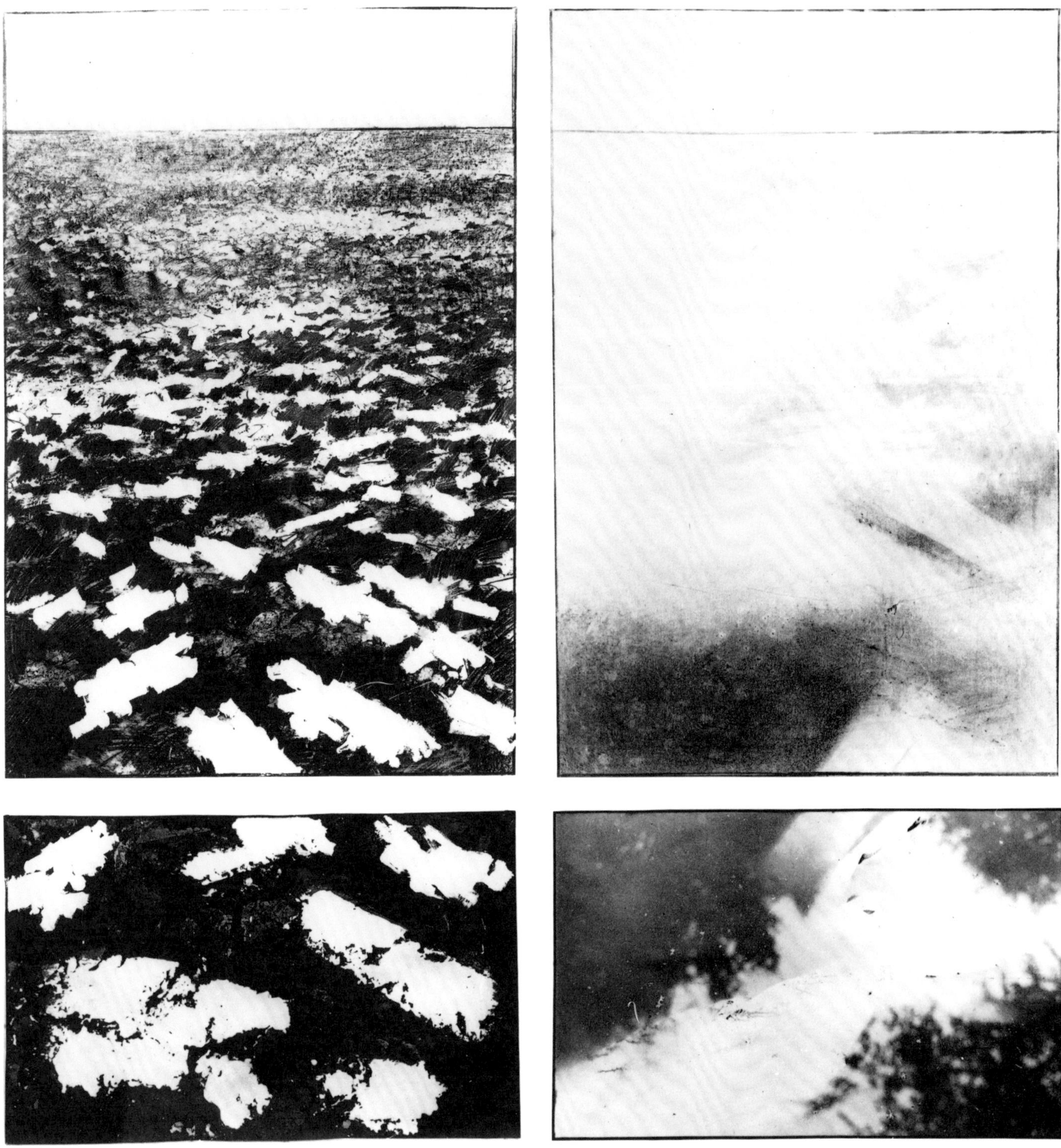

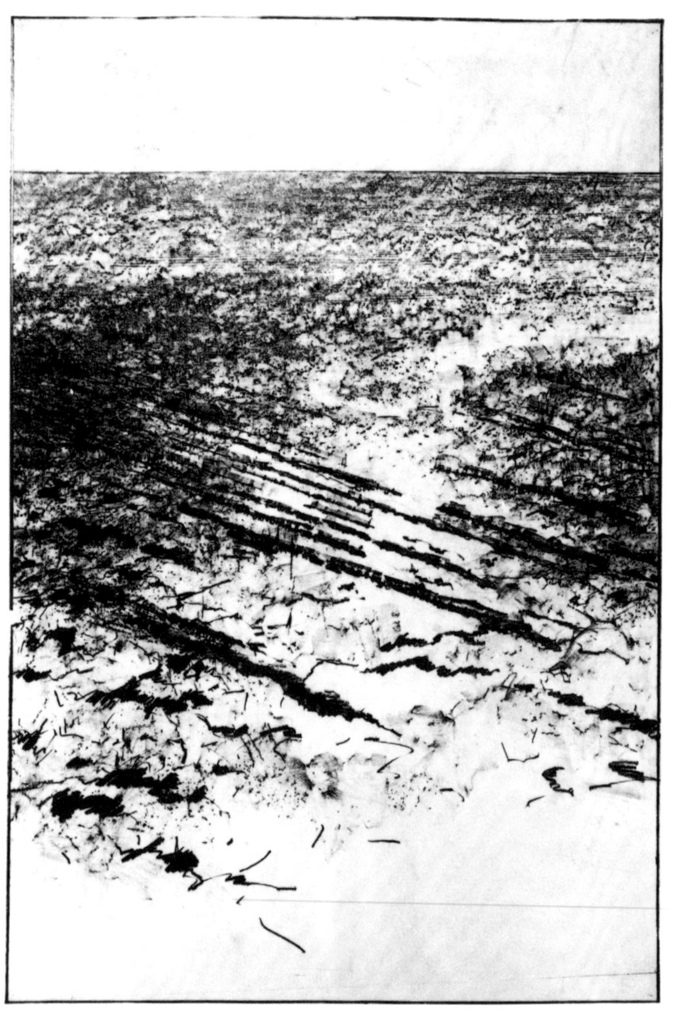
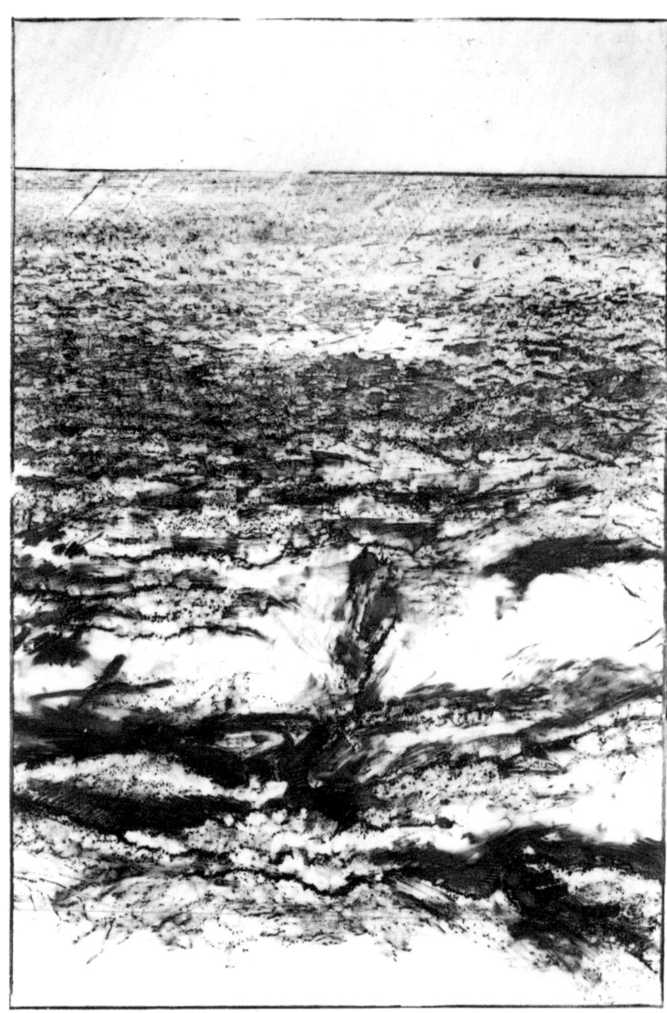
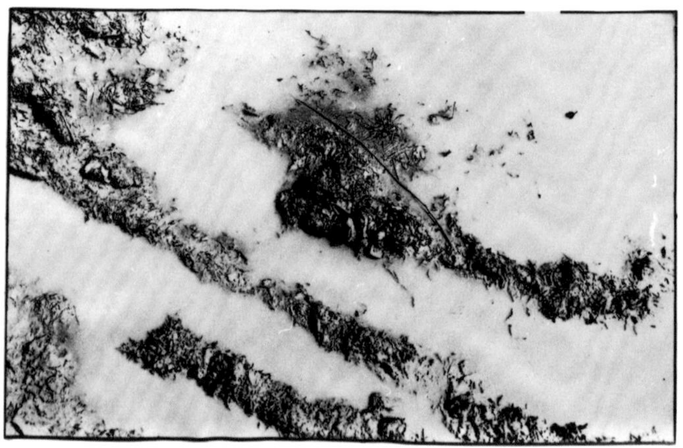
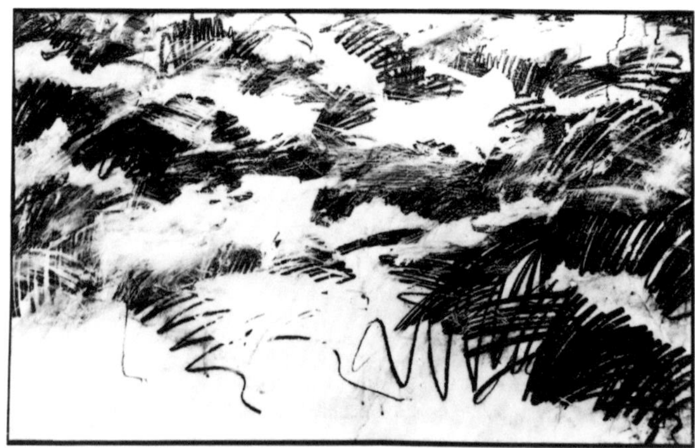

Drawing is a noisy process. The noises of mark-making somehow resonate back through the drawing. The marks hold their noise. It is a kind of residue that operates between action and representation, a debris that edges in between the marks and gaps revealed, echoing the frictions and fictions of things drawn across a surface, in pursuit of a subject. Noise is information lost in the process of translation: a residue which will not change state and cannot be reorganised. In the case of drawing, residue occurs as the process moves through action, onto mark and representation. The order inherent in the drawing always edges towards chaos.

Photography does not have this residue. There is always a real sense of silence. Perhaps this is why I find photographs so hard to look at: they are so overtly visual. The quick click of the shutter and the subsequent processes hardly amount to noise; these are a tightly formulated set of procedures with little room for extraneous activity. Nothing is casual, nothing is improvised. Even on the level of representation the information provided is densely packed with few pauses in it. There is no room for hearsay, no gossip; everything is in place. What is there is really represented, and nothing is extra.

Drawing is rooted not in what is perceived, but in the act of mark-making, which patterns, arrests, and fixes. What is registered is primarily activity: the marks and traces that constitute this activity are a series of stops and starts, of inter-acting gestures, punctuated by gaps – which all precede any notion of objective representation. Only after this activity has been exposed through doing, may we ask what else the marks may go on to represent. Photography does not have this foundation, for what is initially presented there is a world, like Cezanne's 'without gaps', a surface textured with a basic grain, and modulated within a tonal framework. The parts all serve the same function, i.e. to be receptive to whatever light falls on them. This is a democratic procedure in which each part has the potential to receive more or less light, and where a change to one part is a change to the whole.

First published in *Field Series 1978*, Nigel Greenwood Inc Ltd, London, 1979

In this sense, the first ground of the photography, the film, is a sophisticated surface already primed with reference. This basic difference between the loaded ground of the film and the blank ground of the drawing distinguishes the two processes: one is reductive and the other is primarily accumulative. To begin with the photograph is a decision to leave something out; with the drawing it is a decision to put something in. The photograph is potentially as complete as it will ever be the moment it is taken, and subsequent developing and printing are commentaries on that initial action. Light patterns the film (negative), and this in turn patterns the paper, effecting a transfer from negative to positive, which is a direct translation as used in any conventional printing process. The photograph is at its most random when it is first taken; subsequent processes order it, each tightening up on the preceding one. Drawing's method is self-evolving continually with a potential to discontinue, since it emerges from an infinity of possible marks. Each mark is unique and can influence or ignore any preceding one, so determining its own contribution. Thus the drawing arrives at its own destiny.

There is a sense of authenticity within a photograph because it locates the photographer as well as its subject. The camera's perspective pinpoints the position of the photographer even as it describes the scene. The one locates the other. To change perspective is to change the location of the photographer. A broader perspective, a multi-view, can only come out of changing frames of reference, i.e. shifting locations. Place is fixed in time and time is held in place. Occasion becomes a very tight specific, and thus highly authentic. This verification of time and space, this ability to specify, make the photograph so substantial a means of documentation. The photograph contains extensive cross-references and clues which indicate its authenticity. Conversely, a drawing can-not document an occasion. It can comment on it, reveal a sense of it, but its inability to verify time in place and place in time prevents the emergence of anything even resembling a fact. The closest the drawing can get to locating the fact of place is in the map, which, through scale, conveys proportions and relationships outside of time. Beyond this restricted use, drawing is always an approximation, always in a state of probability, for speculation and improvisation forever get in the way. Sense of place comes only from location of place. The tendency towards a multi-perspective constantly relocates the drawing in the same way that time is distorted through anticipation and remembrance. The drawing cannot reproduce anything accurately (least of all itself).

Drawing and photography are like landscape in that they are able to expose and obscure, reveal and conceal. They can erode and produce an image, or reveal abstractions, or reduce further to expose new ground, new relationships. "It rains, it snows, it paints" (Buren). It draws and takes photographs too. These activities also pattern, arrest, and fix, like rain into puddles of water or falling snow into drifts. Photography and drawing are like the agents of land erosion breaking down and rebuilding surfaces. From drops of rain (individual moments of chaos), rainfall collects itself into an ordered whole, transforming surfaces, and establishing a new grain that mirrors the overall oneness of falling rain. This is a precarious co-existence of order and chaos, where singular drops splashing down onto a surface build up to flowing water that washes away sheets of soil and excavates gullies and grooves.

It has been estimated that the impact of a violent storm can blast more than a hundred tons of soil per acre into the air. Such displacement is never seen, but sensed, and the surface changes record it. Here in the rain prints, in the saturated soil, in the mud-flow, are held the clues that graphically reflect the actions of past events. And through these, the grains and lines, the textures and tones, there emerges a patterning of representation. These patterns describe the profiles and horizons of evidence and limits of actions. Substance grows out of the fields and aggregates that patterns describe, and out of the distance between action and consequence. David Smith said that the earth's surface depth does not seem important, since depth is visually inaccessible. What is important is pattern, the traces of interactions, the patterns of nature in relation to those of man. They are always there, always discernible on the surface of the things that they help to constitute and describe, defining the areas of activity, the fields of drawing and projection. In the collivial deposits, the talus accumulations, the scarring and sealing of etched surfaces, a landscape is codified: so likewise are the drawing and the photograph in the marks, smudges, tones, grains and gaps.

Robert Smithson wrote of the "vanishing, vanishing horizon", that far and always so elusive horizon of landscape. As you move towards it, it recedes, and disappears, to reveal a new horizon. Never to be stood on or finally located, it has to be continually relocated and redefined. To zoom in closer, in an attempt to find it, is only to change the problem. As fields disappear, furrows appear; as furrows are walked into, clods of earth are isolated. Moving in still closer, evidence of frost-shattering from continuous freezing and thawing may show itself, or signs of sediment relocation from rain washing the soil from the surface are revealed. From one order to another chaos. The landscape moves continually from horizon to grain, from where it might end to what it might be. A transition, restless, and at times reckless. A ground that is inconsistent, that at any moment may shift its inclination, may swerve and tilt, bank and bend, in order to prevent the concrete, the irrefutable. Any kind of foothold is on shifting soil, whose gradient may have to be climbed over or slid down. In such uncertain terrain crevices may in turn expand into crevasses, or contract into hair-line seams almost too fine to be seen. These seams may turn out to be flow-lines, directional indicators of a more fluid state, describing the emergence of a new grain, as yet another change takes place.

Here is the constant conflict, Mondrian's ideal of horizontal versus vertical, of unification versus isolation. "Landscape is either flat or it is sloping" (K. E. Sawyers). By far the largest proportion of the earth's land surface is on a slope of less than five degrees. Water, wind, temperature change and organic growth, activated by gravity ceaselessly flatten the land. Duchamp sensed the centre of gravity being somewhere in the middle of the stomach, but to me it seems to be everywhere. Permeating the whole body, it is in everything, eroding and redistributing in search of an ideal state, a state encouraged by the sedimentation of the earth. In this flow of things there is no cessation, no inertia, just endless movement, displacing, distributing and locating, yet again to displace. This sense of movement, this contradictory coexistence, this continuity and discontinuity, forever uniting and dividing, cementing and fracturing, rejects definition. Attempts to search for either sublime or irrefutable structures, for either metaphysical or possible systems – like the crazy perfections of Borges' cartographers in *On Exactitude in Science*, where all is mapped, and in the end all is map – lead nowhere.

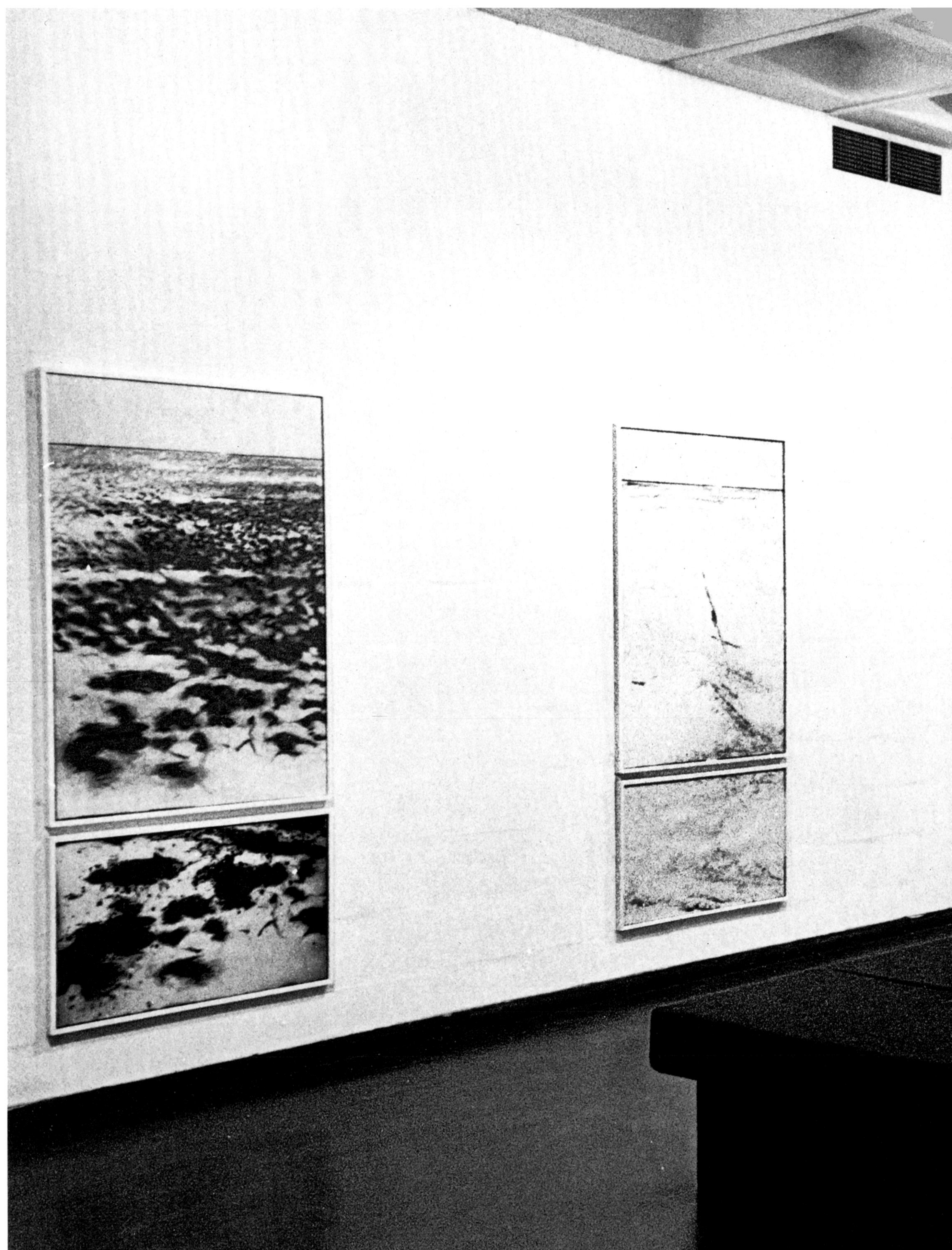

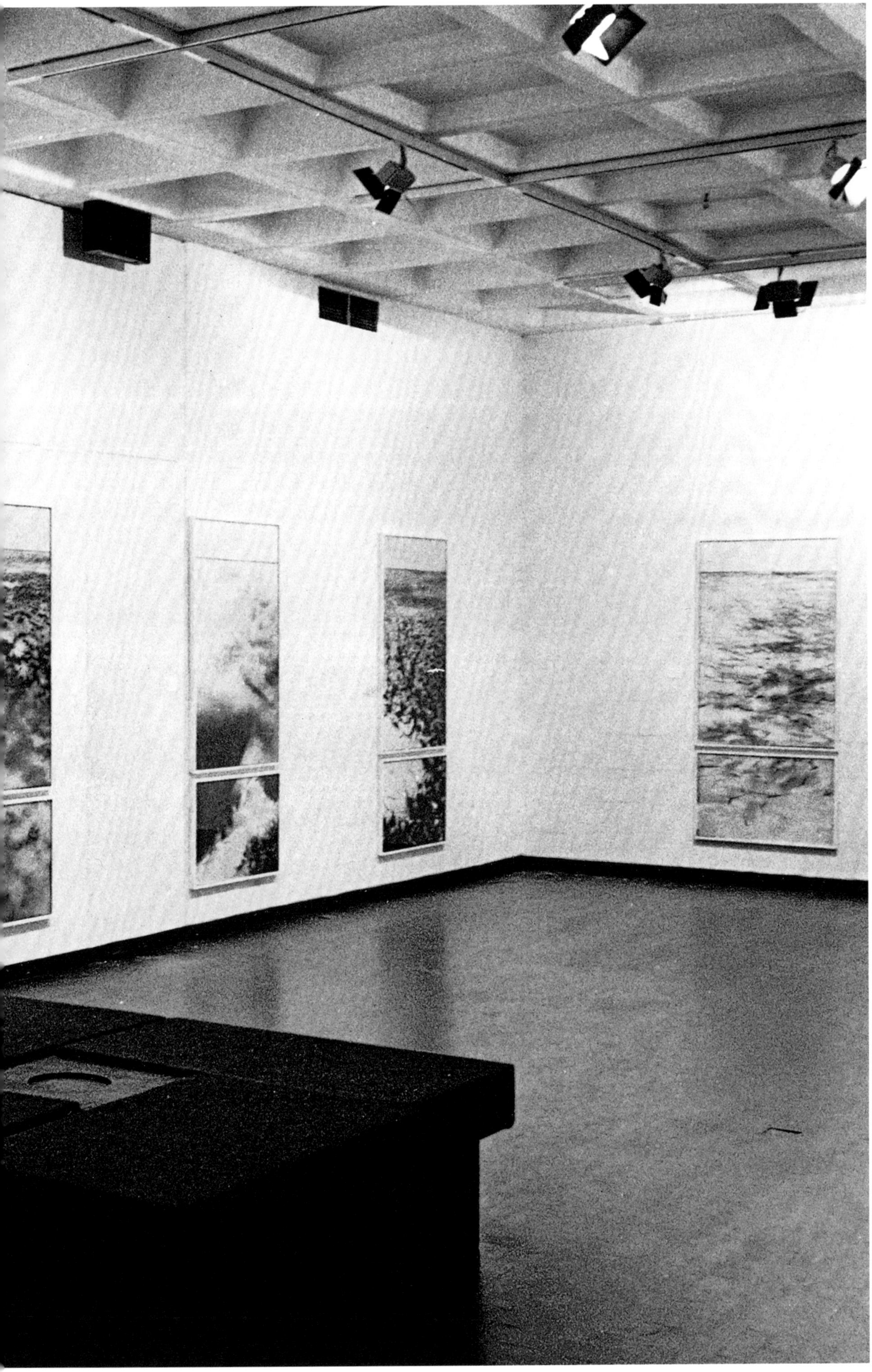

Fields, Waterfalls and Birds, (Field Series), Arnolfini Gallery, Bristol, 1980

foreground by resembling the drawing's texture. Inclined by this proximity to apply the same rules of interpretation to the photograph as to the drawing, the viewer is forced to reassess the validity of those rules when the difference in medium becomes apparent. As in the 'Sand and Sea' series such readjusted assumptions are subject to further revision when the viewer becomes aware that what appears to be a photograph of landscape is often a photograph of a drawing in the landscape.

One of the 'Field' series diptychs (they do not have individual titles) plays on a likeness between the drawing and photographic components. The application of an eraser to the lower parts of the drawing creates a blurred, bleached effect which is taken up by a black-and-white photograph of thin ice through which strands of grass poke, as though the whitish ice were an erasure of the darker grass. In another of the works, the likeness between drawing and photograph is presented as a form of double entendre. The photograph, which resembles the drawing above it, proves on closer inspection to be a photograph of a drawing. Contrast heightens towards the bottom of the drawing, suggesting a layer of tilled top-soil, while the high-contrast photograph below it shows a similar drawing placed into a field, its pencil marks partially obscured by a light covering of snow which corresponds to the white of the paper. The stark tonal contrasts both reflect the drawing and reproduce it. Submitting to these complex entanglements between different modes of representation, the viewer registers ambiguities which confound familiar representational tropes, such as that of the horizon line around which the works are structured.

The narrow, upright format of the 'Field' series, divided by the horizon line and the gap between drawing and photograph, recalls the scale and composition of a mid-period Mark Rothko painting, such as *Untitled* (ca. 1950–52), in the Tate collection, in which the canvas is divided into hovering zones of colour with horizontal junctures. The lilac panel at the bottom of *Untitled* corresponds, in shape, to the photograph at the base of a work from the 'Field' series. But it is Rothko's late series of acrylic paintings, known as the 'Black Paintings' (1969–70), in which he explored the potential of offsetting a horizontal juncture, which registers as a horizon line, with a painterly idiom which refutes pictorial illusion. Despite their invocation of the tradition of sublime landscape painting, these are Rothko's flattest, most ironic, even nihilistic works. The horizon line proffers a visual cue which is doubly subverted: by placing a dark zone above a lighter greyish zone (reverse the zones, and the landscape reading becomes irresistible), and by painterly activity which ignores or contradicts the horizon reading, refusing to supply detail which would flesh out the two zones as earth and sky, and confirm the spatial recession the juncture intimates.

The comparison of a work from the 'Field' series to a Mark Rothko painting has broader implications in that the late-1970s is the point in McKeever's development when early-conceptual rationalism is met at least half-way by the influence of 20th-century modernist abstraction, particularly US Abstract Expressionism, with its figure-high scales and explicit gesturalism. Whereas the conceptual tradition promotes rationalism and relativism, modernist abstraction asks of its viewer a submission to a categorical statement, a non-empirical assertion. These are antitheses, with the former largely arising out of its rejection of the latter. The 'Field' series is designed to explore where and how belief surmounts reason and reason deconstructs belief, as Rothko's 'Black Paintings' simultaneously negate and confirm the illusionistic depth of a compositional structure which comprehends the sublimity of traditional landscape painting.

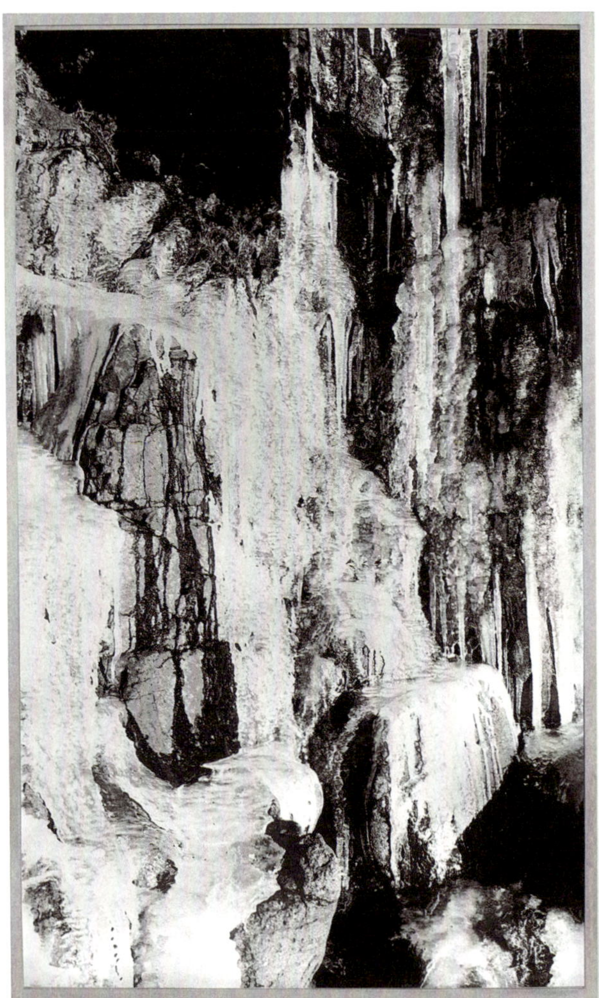

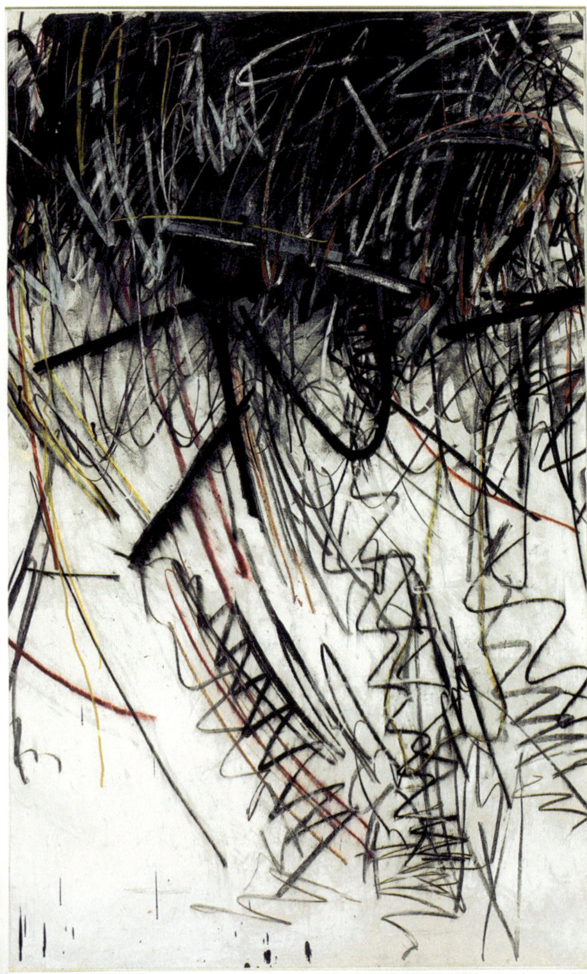

In 1974, McKeever left St Katherine's Dock to take a studio in a newly-converted complex on Martello Street, which runs along the border of London Fields in Hackney. He was among several artists who moved between the sites, most of whom were working in a conceptual vein. But by the end of the 1970s, several abstract painters – including, for example, Gary Wragg and James Faure Walker – had also moved in, forming a culture that was torn between conceptualism and painting. McKeever recalls straddling the two camps, unassimilated by either, his work 'too messy for the conceptualists, and too dry for the painters'[2].

The two leading British art magazines of the period, Art Monthly and Artscribe – both first published in 1976 – reflected this duality. Some of the painters at Martello Street, not including McKeever, were among those who formed Artscribe, and went on to contribute to it. Jack Wendler, the American publisher of Art Monthly, ran a commercial art gallery in London in the early 1970s, with a programme which included many significant figures of early conceptual art, from mainland Europe, Britain, and the USA. Art Monthly, the magazine he co-founded, reflected that emphasis. According to its present editor, Patricia Bickers, 'the inaugural issue contained an undertaking "to provide informed coverage on contemporary art and the issues that surround it", a stance that contrasted sharply with the then dominant Anglo-American formalist view of art, derived largely from Clement Greenberg, that argued for the aesthetic, political and economic autonomy of art.'[3] She notes that Artscribe, in contrast, 'was very much biased towards painting, being largely written by painters for painters as well as being, at least in the beginning, edited by painters.'[4]

While on a residency in the German city of Nürnberg in 1982, McKeever began to compose *Black and White ... Or How to Paint with a Hammer*, a short text he published as a

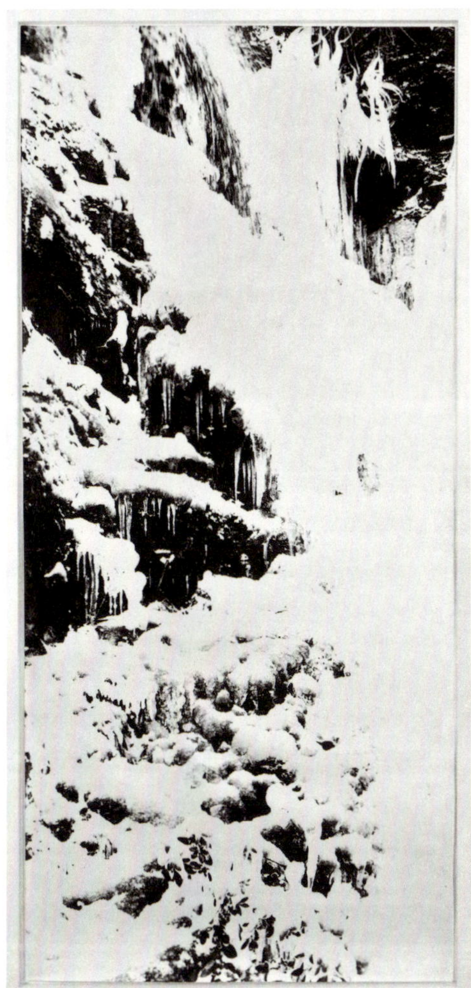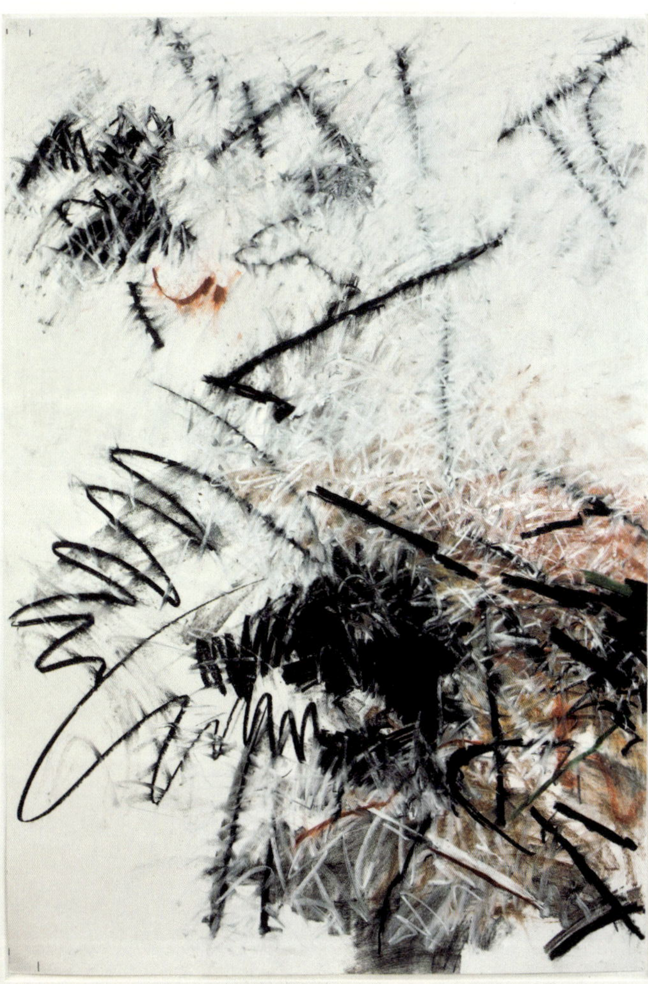

pamphlet in conjunction with his exhibition at Matts Gallery in London in the autumn of that year. The text consists of rhetorical imperatives, impassioned exclamations, and private anecdotes that combine into a commentary on the conflict between what McKeever describes as 'the neatness of the conceptual, photo-based position, and the more formless and belief-based position of the painter'.[5] The text is characterised by natural metaphors for art, one of which might stand as an epigraph to the 'Waterfalls' series (1979): 'I remember standing under a waterfall, framing it in the camera and thinking of a Barnett Newman painting.'[6] The sentence conflates three, distinct frames of reference – nature, abstract painting and photography. Nature is represented by a phenomenon characterised by movement, but translated into media – painting and photography – which are still. Stasis and flow – those of a representational image, a natural event, and an image as a distillation of that event – are the terms around which the 'Waterfalls' coalesce. This is the last of McKeever's series in which early-conceptual forms dominate, and the first to have developed out of a working process which would become a staple of McKeever's work of the 1980s: a field trip to a remote landscape during which he would produce a series of photographs and drawings, followed by a period of protracted, urban, studio-based gestation. A trip to the Scottish Isle of Skye in January 1979 was the departure for 'Waterfalls'.

A trompe l'oeil element, structuralistically highlighting a work's media, is carried over from previous series. The photographic half of the diptychs shows a frozen waterfall. Flow is a waterfall's essence, and is of course frozen by a photograph. By photographing waterfalls in a frozen state, McKeever makes the camera's imposition of stasis self-reflexively tautological. Even the word 'freeze', in this context, has a double meaning – both literal and figurative. The conjunction of black-and-white photograph and

Waterfalls No.5, 1979

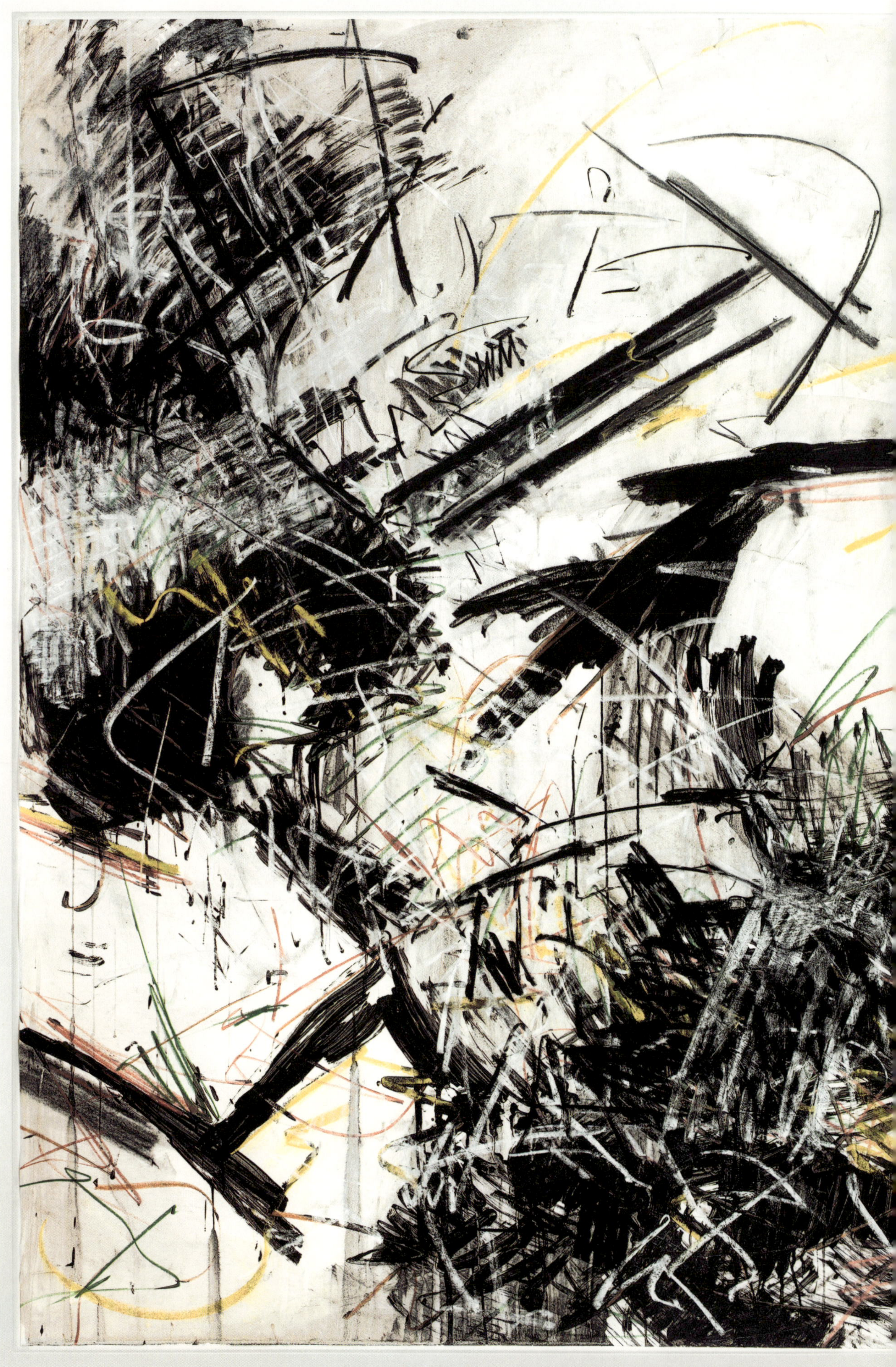

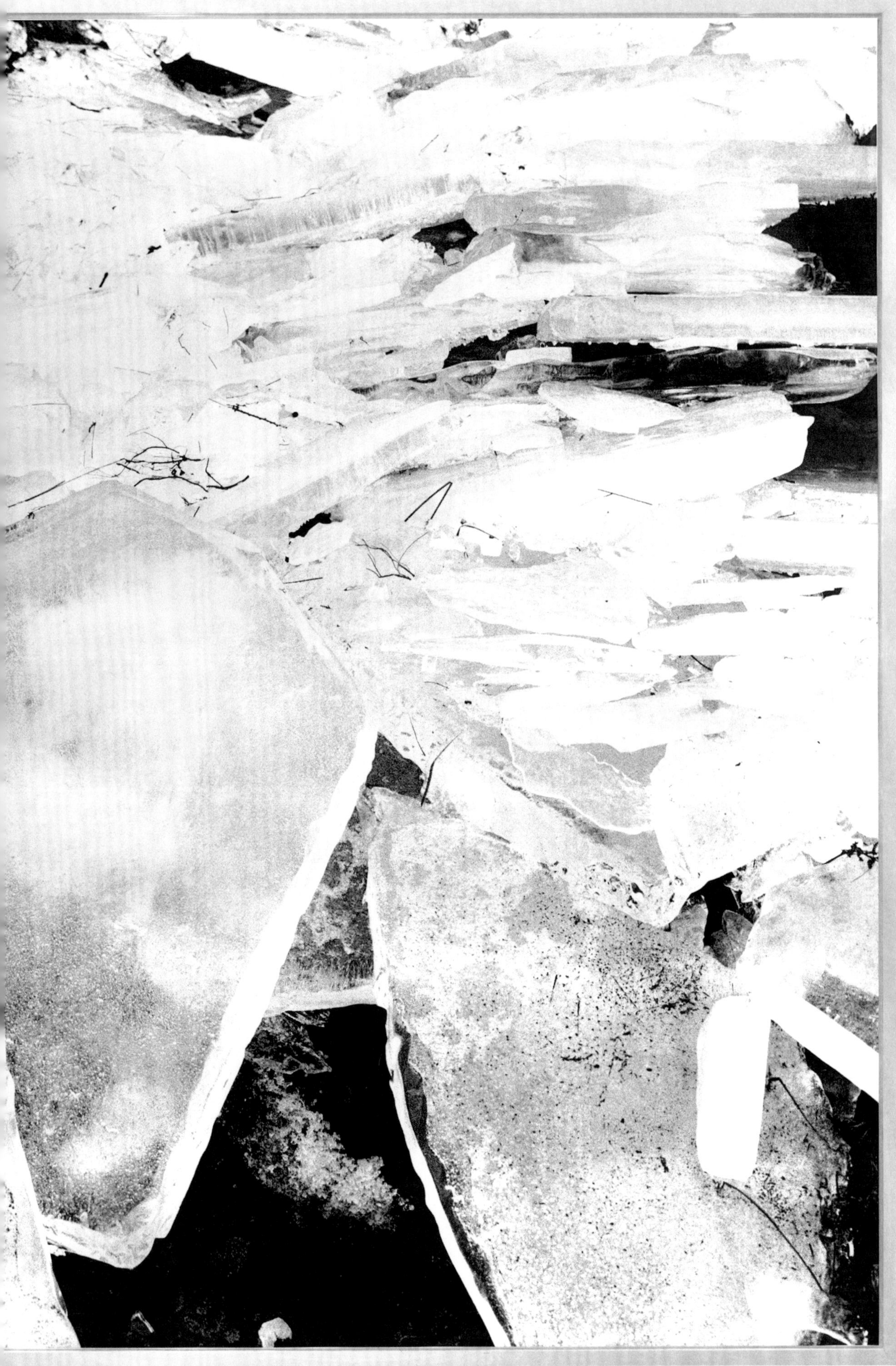

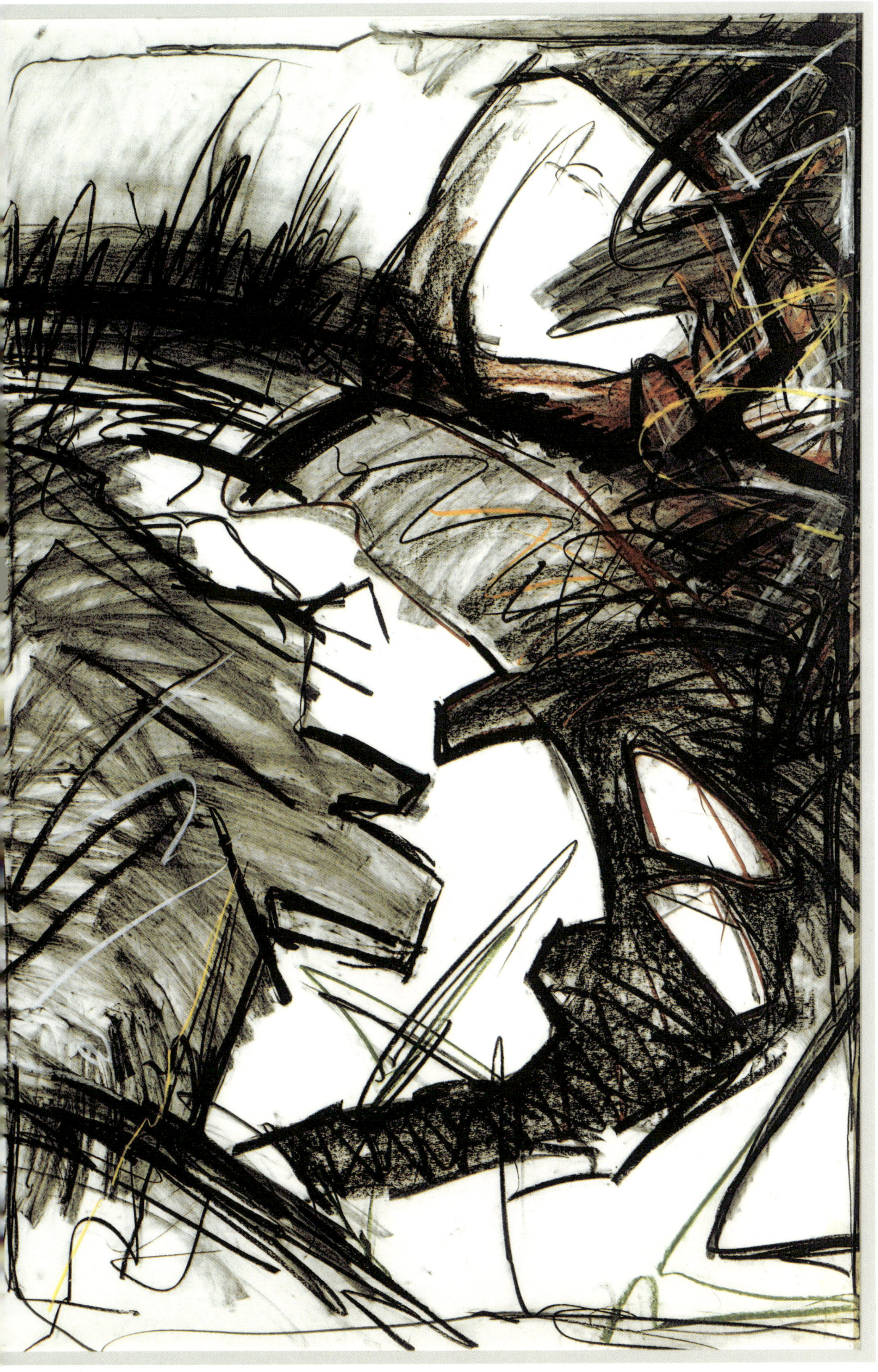

Waterfalls No.7, 1979

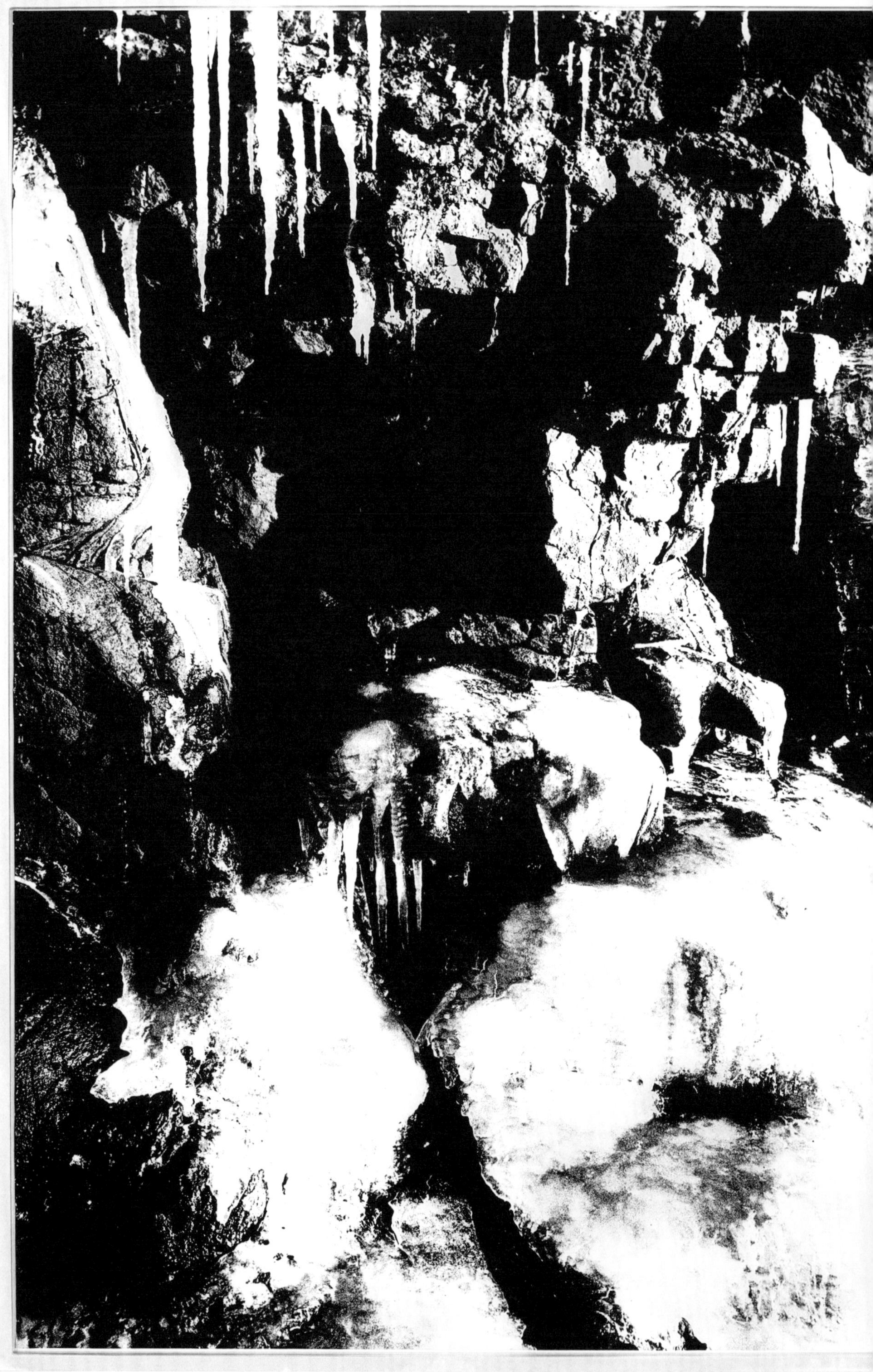

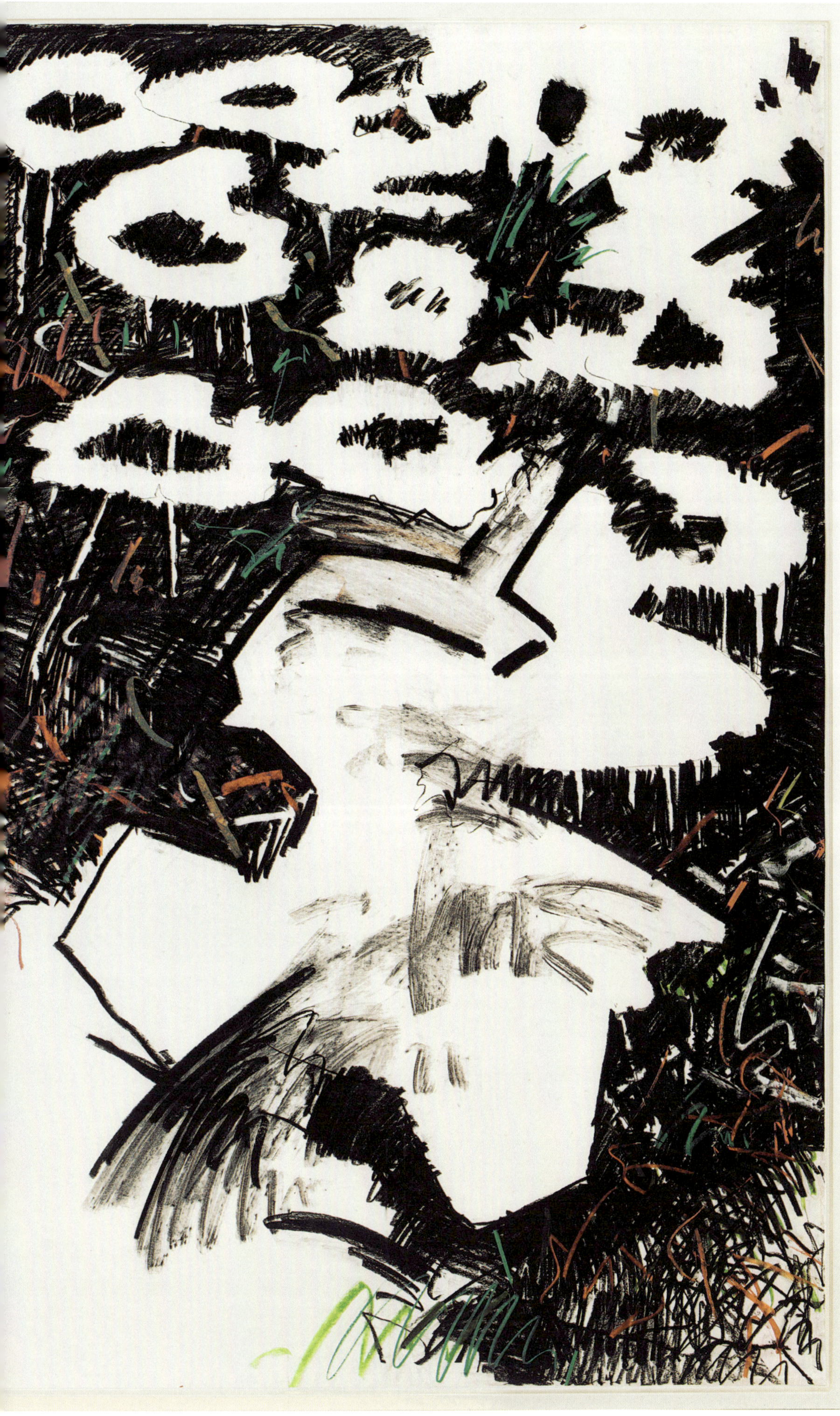

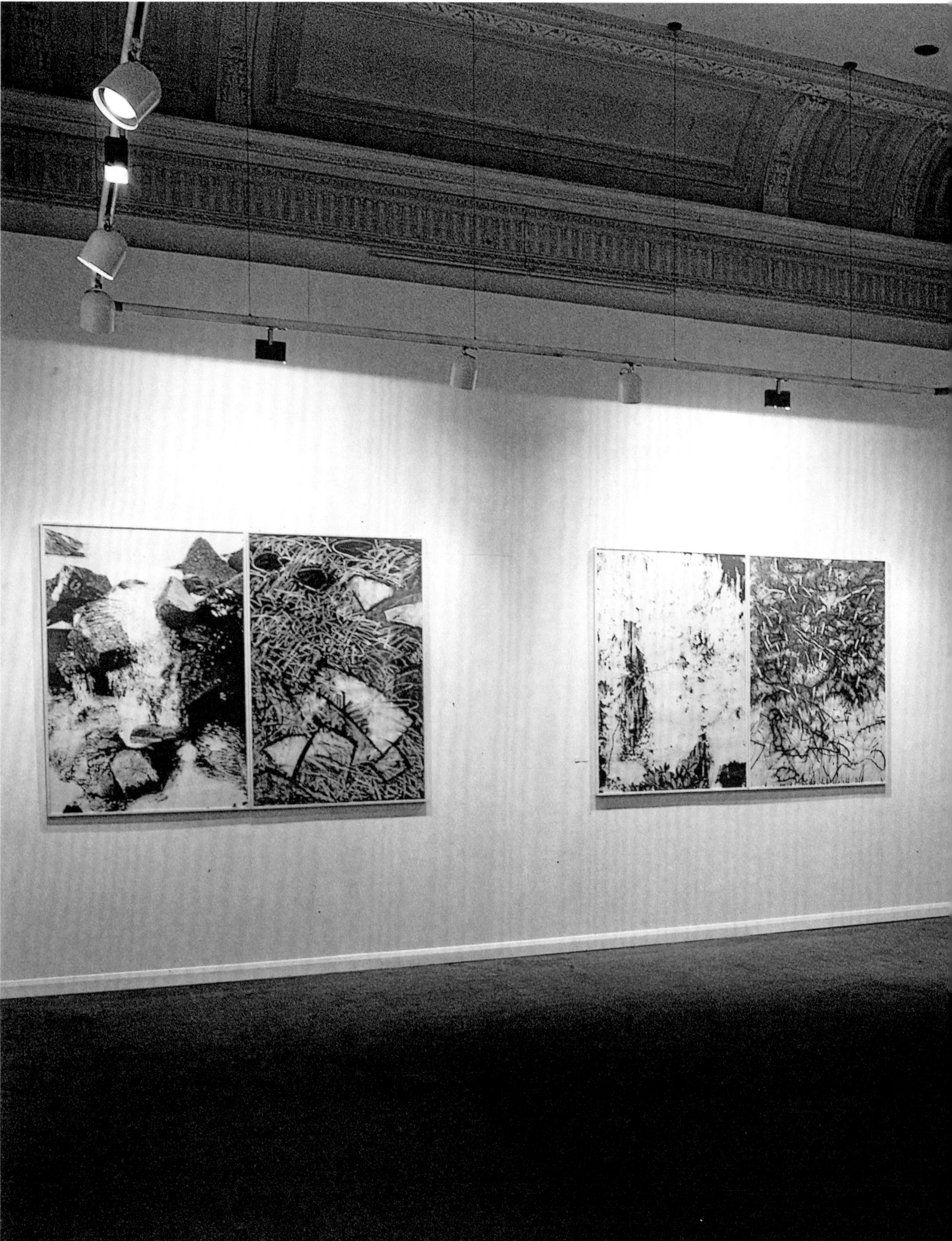

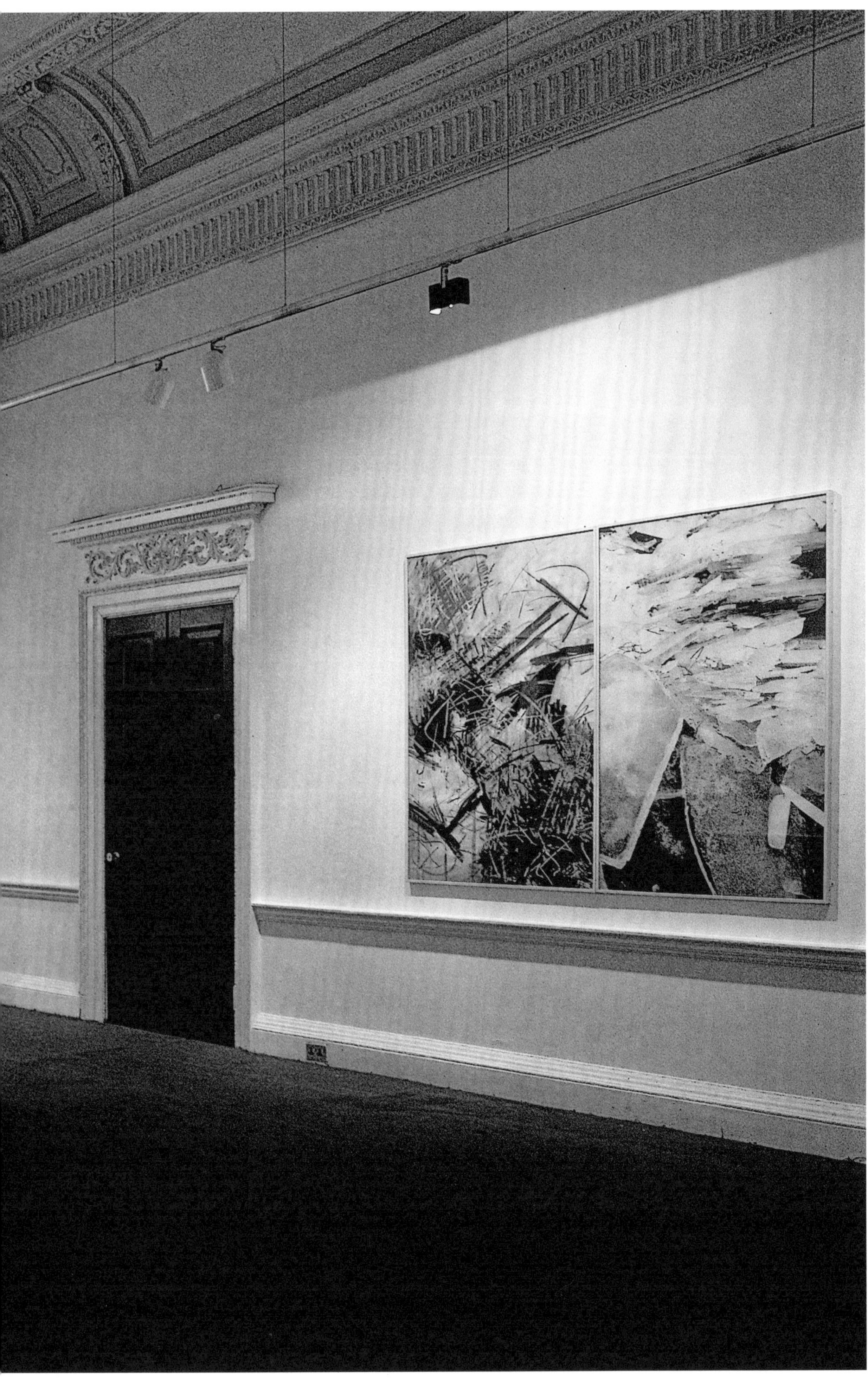

*Fields, Waterfalls
and Birds*, (Waterfalls),
Institute of
Contemporary
Art, London, 1980

charcoal drawing – both over two metres high – places into dialectical opposition not only the varying lengths of time each encapsulates, but alternative positions taken to art-making: one 'belief-based'; the other 'conceptual-objective'. But these positions are not left in a simply antithetical relation to each other. McKeever's method is to erode the polarities of a binary structure by exposing likeness within contrasts. Although the drawings switch between representational and abstract idioms, both drawing and photograph are empirical modes. The methodology pursued by the diptychs is an empirically representational one in relation to the primary experience of the landscape they represent. Each medium produces a metaphor for painting, a medium which is absent but everywhere invoked. McKeever claimed, 'I think that the Waterfall pieces are to a large extent about painting although they present themselves as a drawing and photo[graph] ... They are an attempt to say something about the nature of painting as an activity'.[7]

'Empirical' implies *a posteriori* knowledge, based on primary experience, but also suggests an experimental process of gathering knowledge. Both meanings apply to the 'Waterfalls' series despite McKeever's concern with eliciting abstract qualities from both photograph and drawing by emphasising correspondences between each and painterly abstraction, a non-empirical form. Abstraction, applied to a representational template, may have its own counter-representational function, connoting the resistance of reality to being assimilated to the demands of representation, for example by positing the strain of a still representation's attempt to capture a moving subject. In Roland Barthes' terms, it qualifies the 'real' as 'unintelligible'[8].

The drawn and photographic panels of *Waterfall No.2* (1979) are of unequal width but identical height, initiating a dialectic based on a statement of equivalence which is simultaneously qualified as partial. The congruence of the two panels is based on their identical height and similarly disposed tonalities, while the binary juxtaposition between their media is a form of diametrical incongruence. Congruence and incongruence between the panels are proposed, only for each to be rejected by the other. Likeness is undeniable: the narrower, drawn panel shares with the photograph to its left a preponderance of black, gathering in intensity towards the top right corner. But the dark, upper area of the drawing is a tangle of vigorous strokes of black pastel that make no attempt to depict the corresponding area in the photograph: a block of shadows behind a shelf of hanging stalagmites. Indeed, according to the terms of McKeever's dialectic – which comprehends a state of democracy between the media, granting each its autonomy – for one medium to imitate the other would be a form of submission. And yet, the drawing's cascading scribbles of pastel, charcoal and chalk invite a comparison with the frozen progress of ice down the vertical length of the photograph. Our inability to establish a direct, mimetic connection between the two panels leads to a perceptual default to less literal relations. The artist's physical energy, manifested as a still trace in the drawing, corresponds to the natural energy of water flow, frozen to ice, in the photograph. In each panel, therefore, energy – either that of human or landscape, both of which, of course, are aspects of nature – resolves itself as patterning.

Impelled to consider, by way of these comparisons, how each panel – and the medium it deploys and represents – formalises information, the viewer is irresistibly drawn into a structuralistic comparison between photography and drawing. The white of the drawing is that of the unmarked paper ground; while the white of the photograph is where its own paper ground has registered the least exposure of light, inversely corresponding to the lightest parts of the image

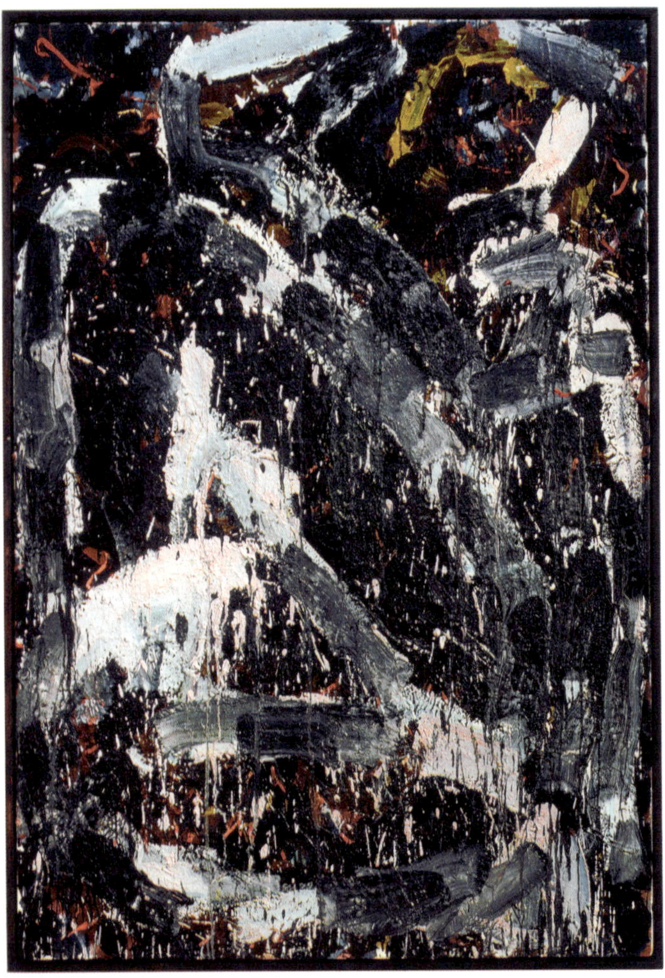

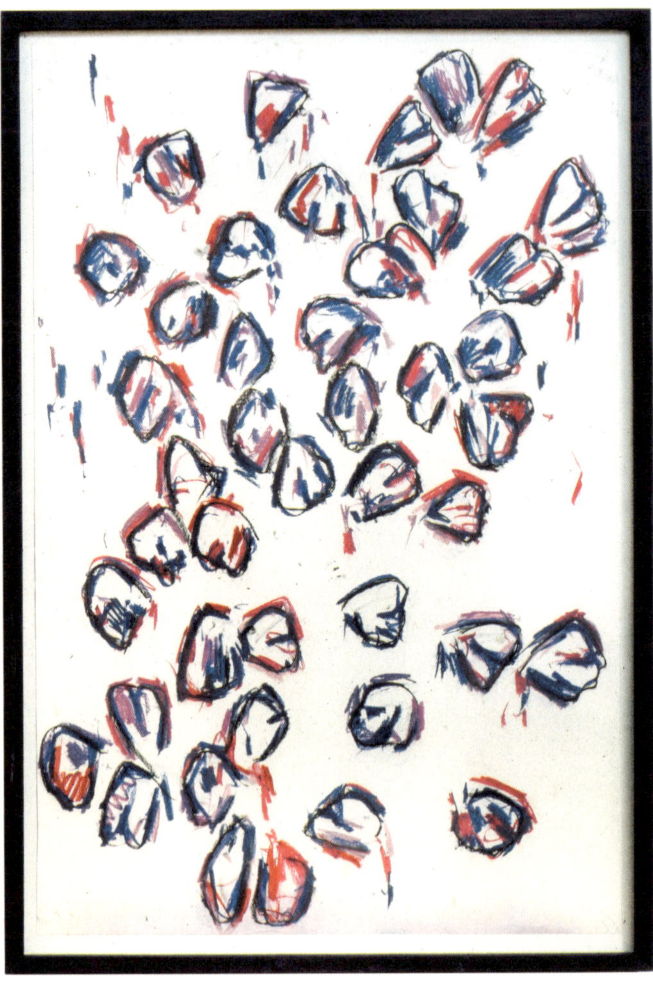

because it has been exposed through a negative. We realise that light, in both media, represents absence. McKeever's dialectic has taken us from contradicting the simple mimesis between panels which their combination may have led us to expect, to likeness of a more metaphorical or conceptual nature, which nonetheless brings us back to the fundamental material properties of the respective media.

In the 'Waterfalls' series the two parts of a diptych, although they may be a photograph and a drawing, are synonymous with photography and painting, and establish a dialectic between them, one which has evolved into an artistic tradition of its own through the work of Chuck Close, Gerhard Richter, Sigmar Polke, Luc Tuymans, as well as that of younger painters, such as Glenn Brown and Eberhard Haverkost, who emerged in the 1990s using painting techniques ultimately deriving from Richter's photo-paintings. But

whereas such artists proceed from a voluntary entrenchment in the tradition of late-20th century painting, McKeever always approaches the medium as an interloper rather than an initiate. He also differs in his refusal to base a commentary on photography on painting's mimicking of its qualities. However radically he blends the media, he never induces them to forsake their indigenous qualities.

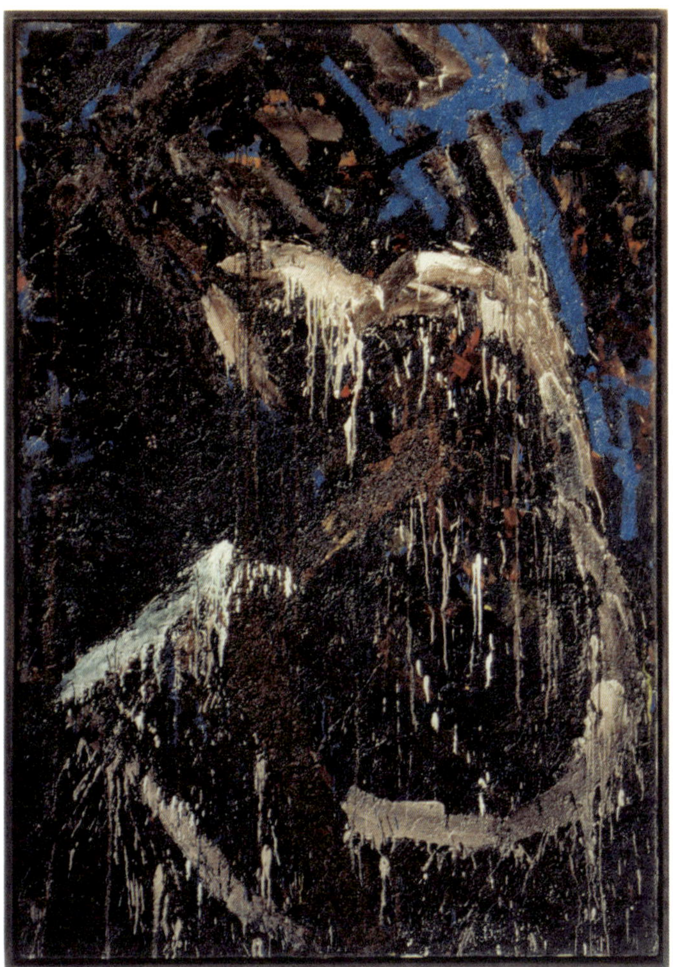

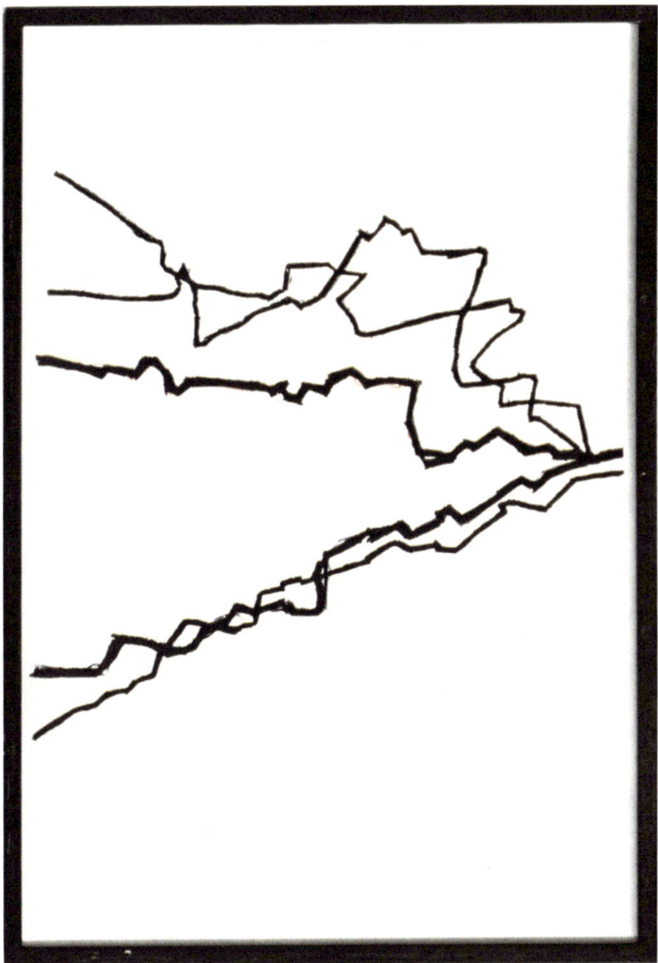

Out of the list of artists above, only Richter's work corresponds to McKeever's in its emphasis on a relativistic splintering of contrasting modes and media. But the sweep of Richter's dry brush over the surface of one of his photo-paintings, agglomerating painterly detail into a metaphor for the instantaneous click of a camera's shutter, places the medium of painting in a deferential relationship to the presumed authority of the photographic image, an imbalance which is only partially redressed by the painting's having qualified and replaced its photographic model. A Chuck Close portrait, with its aggregated pixellisation of painting, or Sigmar Polke's painterly imitation of the Benday dots of half-tone printing, constitutes a corresponding submission. Each idiom suggests, in the very texture of its technique, that the subjectivity inherent in the medium of painting must masquerade under the guise of a photograph's mechanical objectivity if it is to pass muster as authentic in the realm of postmodern image-making.

In maintaining a dialectic in which neither drawing nor photograph cedes its autonomy to the other, the 'Waterfalls' series implicitly critiques painting that assumes the image of photography. But the problem McKeever encountered in holding painting and photography in a relativistic equilibrium without attempting to merge them is that the binary structure of the contrast tends to simplistically polarise the respective qualities of each medium. However assiduously he worked to erode this dynamic from within – by his emphasis on likeness and collusion as much as on contrast – his development in the early 1980s shows him resisting the limitations of a comparative dualism, and its intellectual source, conceptual art's rationalism.

This dilemma resulted in the 'Night Flak' series (1981), produced during an Arts Council residency in Liverpool, and distinguished by its rejection of a photographic component,

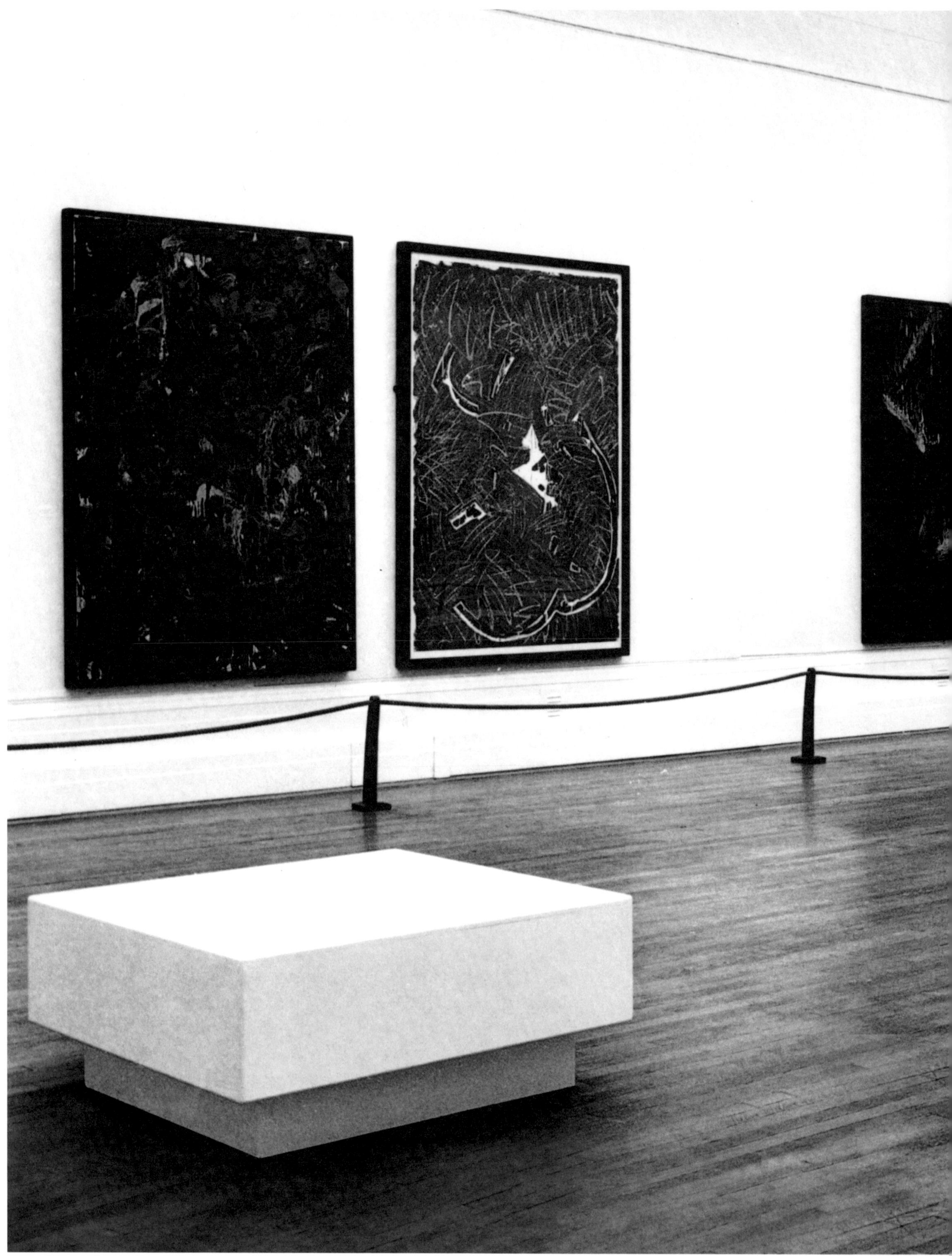

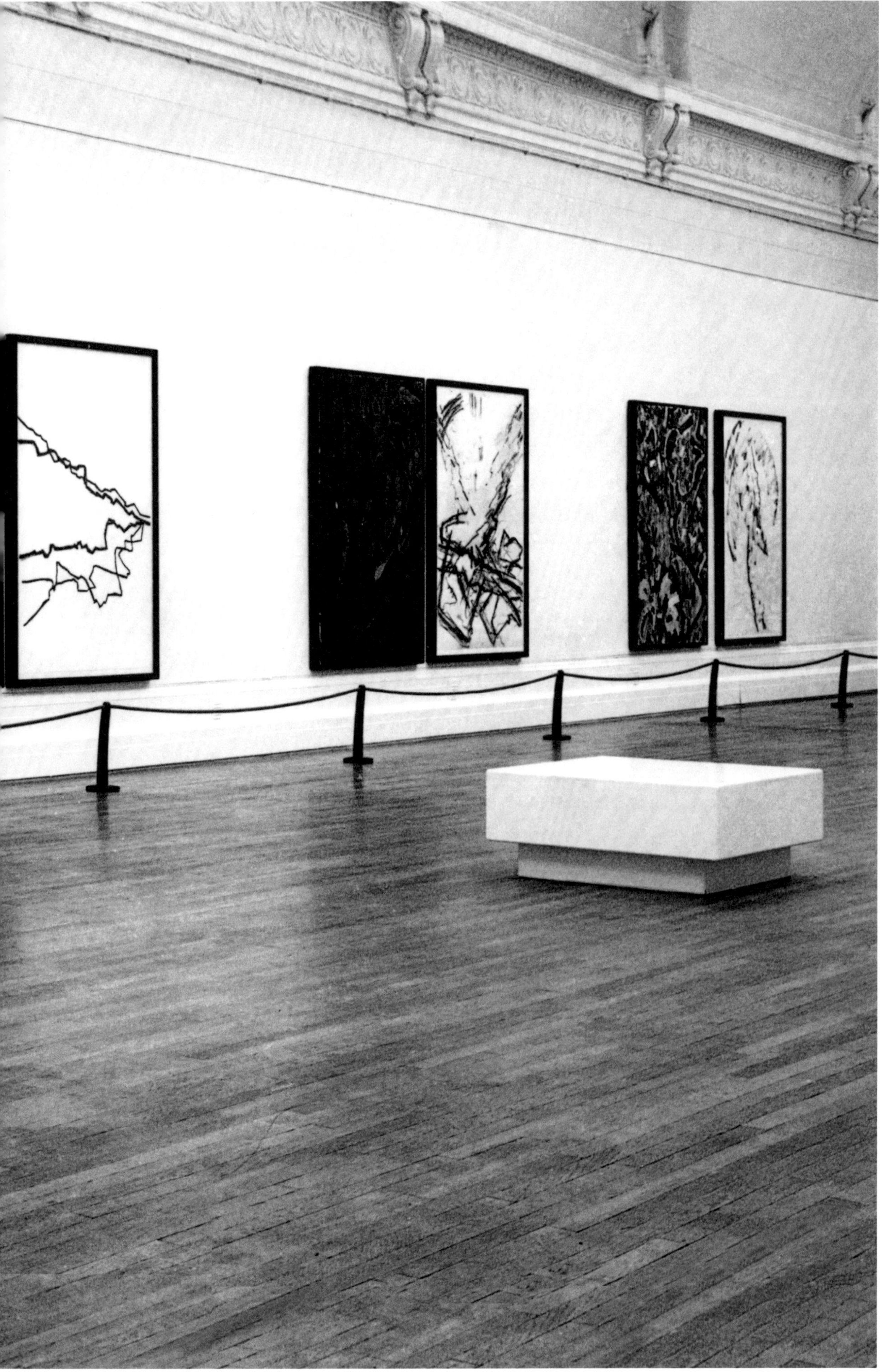

Islands and Night Flak,
(Night Flak), Walker
Art Gallery, Liverpool,
1981

and with it the landscape subject. The photograph's absence emphasises the peculiarity of the role of the landscape motif in McKeever's art. Unlike Richard Long, a landscape artist who emerged during the early-conceptual period using conceptual methods, or John Constable, a painter from the British landscape painting tradition with whose work McKeever has claimed particular affinity, McKeever gives the landscape a tangential and subordinate role. It is a pretext for an artistic process. The periods he spent immersed in the landscape, prior to producing a series of works in his studio, can be understood as blocks of exemplary, unadulterated primary experience upon which an analytical process would be subsequently applied. That application, not the landscape itself, is the work's subject. Landscape is the cue for a narrative, or the context in which it takes place, instead of being the narrative itself.

A comparison might be drawn with the role of landscape in the 'Lights' series (1970–75) by the British painter Michael Andrews (1928–1995). Seven paintings follow the aerial progress of a hot air balloon over various backdrops. Any single painting in the series, considered out of the context, could be considered a work of traditional British landscape painting, in which the representation of landscape, and the political and sociological values its representation confirms or rejects, was paramount. In context, however, the balloon emerges as a symbol of a floating ego, its vulnerable autonomy impacted by the vagaries of the world surrounding it, a self cast adrift within an environment that is by turns hostile, assimilative, and sympathetic. For Andrews, landscape is the frame in which this narrative unfolds, as, in McKeever's art, it is a space in which dynamic processes can be studied. For neither artist is landscape the subject *per se*.

The six 'Night Flak' diptychs demonstrate this distinction by jettisoning the landscape as represented subject, but retaining it in a sense McKeever had broached in the 'Field' series, in which the paper support of the works is conceived of as a terrain his activity traverses, depositing its variable traces. The left panels were painted at night, in an unlit room, allowing McKeever only a sense of touch to guide him, while the right panels were painted in normal, 'sighted' conditions. The left panel of *A Night of Solace in the Dark of Fears* (1981) is a canvas densely encrusted with earth-coloured oil paint that drips upwards, as if the painting were registering the directional disorientation to which McKeever submitted in painting it. The format of the canvases, 213 x 150cm, was determined by estimating the largest area McKeever could reach with his arms outstretched. Painting has been reduced to blind, unconceptualised physical gesture. Only the most inchoate of images emerges from the murk as though to reveal itself more fully would force the tentativeness of touch to succumb to the more powerful impression of sight, and a haptic idiom

to succumb to the more powerful sway of pictorial illusion. By negating the predominating function of sight in the creation of a painting, McKeever converts the canvas into a metaphor for landscape itself rather than its representation.

The right panel, in pastel on paper, is the left's antithesis; spare where it is densely accreted, schematic where it is materialistic, conceptual where it is an effusion of unsublimated gesture. A series of jagged, black pastel lines zigzag across the paper and converge at a midpoint along the right edge. This is the conceptualisation of the picture plane as landscape: rugged terrain formalised as the surface of a map traversed by road routes or contour lines. The dialectical dynamic of the 'Waterfalls' series is retained, while foregoing its explicit contrast between media, because an oil painting and a drawing, although they are different media, are of the same order of artifice. The diptych is reformulated as a form as contingent upon extension as comparison, because we can only define the content of either panel in relation to the other in ambiguous, qualitative terms.

The 'Night Flak' series embodies a desire to pursue a holistic structure that would be less amenable to the binary dichotomies on which conceptual art thrived. Consequentially, the text *Black and White … Or How to Paint with a Hammer*, written the following year, confirms McKeever's intention of conceiving of art as 'an act of faith rather than cool logic'.[9] The subsequent 'Traditional Landscape' series (1982–84) reinstates both the representation of landscape and the photograph which represents it; but by superimposing painting onto a photographic ground, the binary structure of 'Waterfalls' is collapsed into a fluidly integrated whole, in which a single image registers on the viewer before the distinct threads out of which it is woven can be distinguished.

At this point in his development, McKeever's progress can be perceived as a series of incremental steps towards fusing the discrete, constelled components of a conceptual art discourse into a form in which thought is pursued through the agency of immediate, perceptual impact. The argument, the tensions it generates, and their potential reconciliation are to be processed simultaneously. To achieve this fusion, the equilibrium the 'Waterfalls' maintain between painting and photography is thrown off balance. Painting qualifies photograph. This imbalance makes the 'Traditional Landscapes' a decisive step further along an axis that would take McKeever into a pure painting practice by the end of the 1980s. It also indicates a way beyond that point, by formulating his first version of a painting process in which defined painterly gesture qualifies the blur of an underlying tonal ground, a dramatic formal contrast which ultimately replaced that between painting and photography and continues to structure his paintings up to the present.

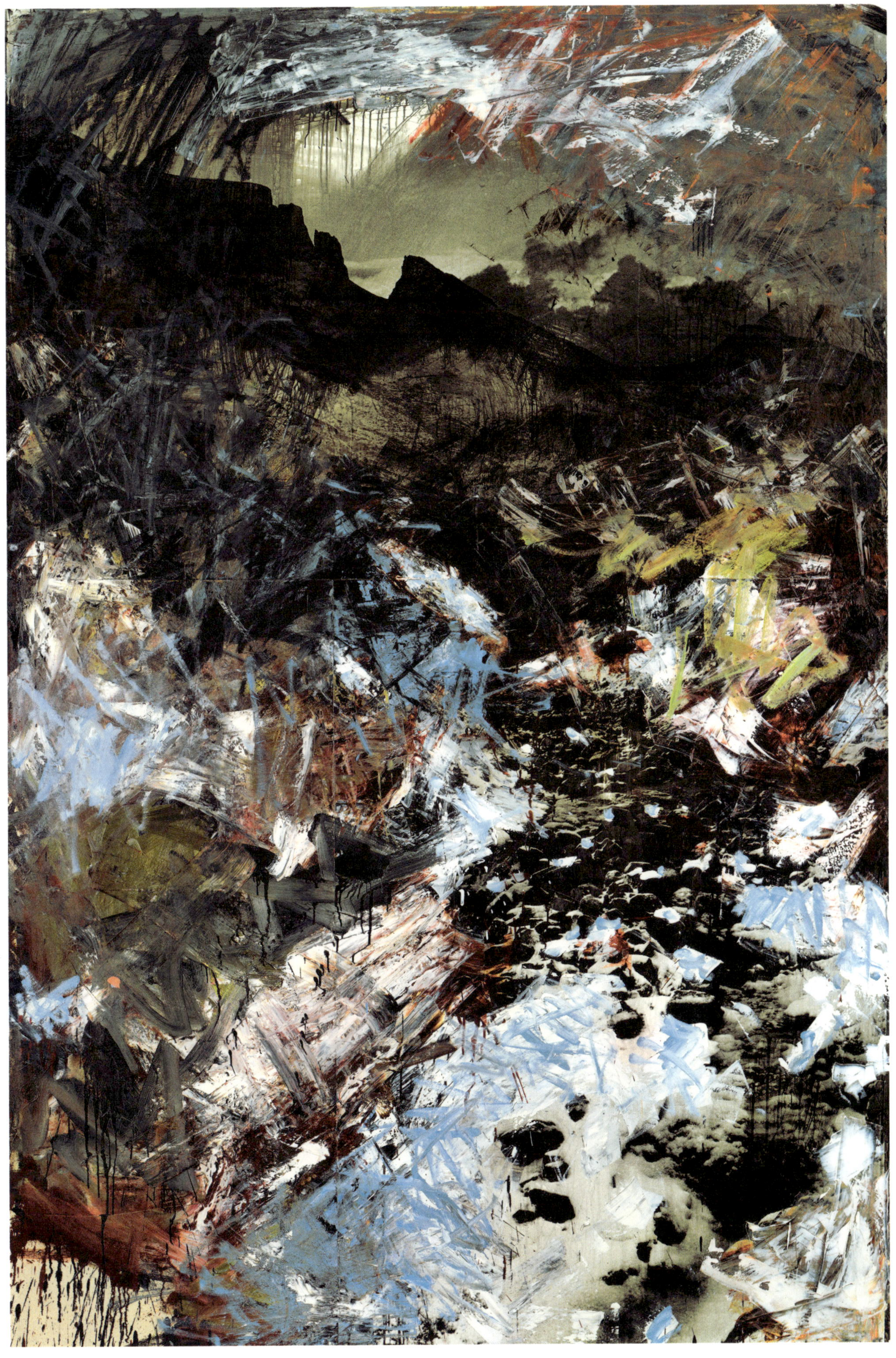

TL 9 Earth of the
Slumbering and Liquid
Trees, 1983

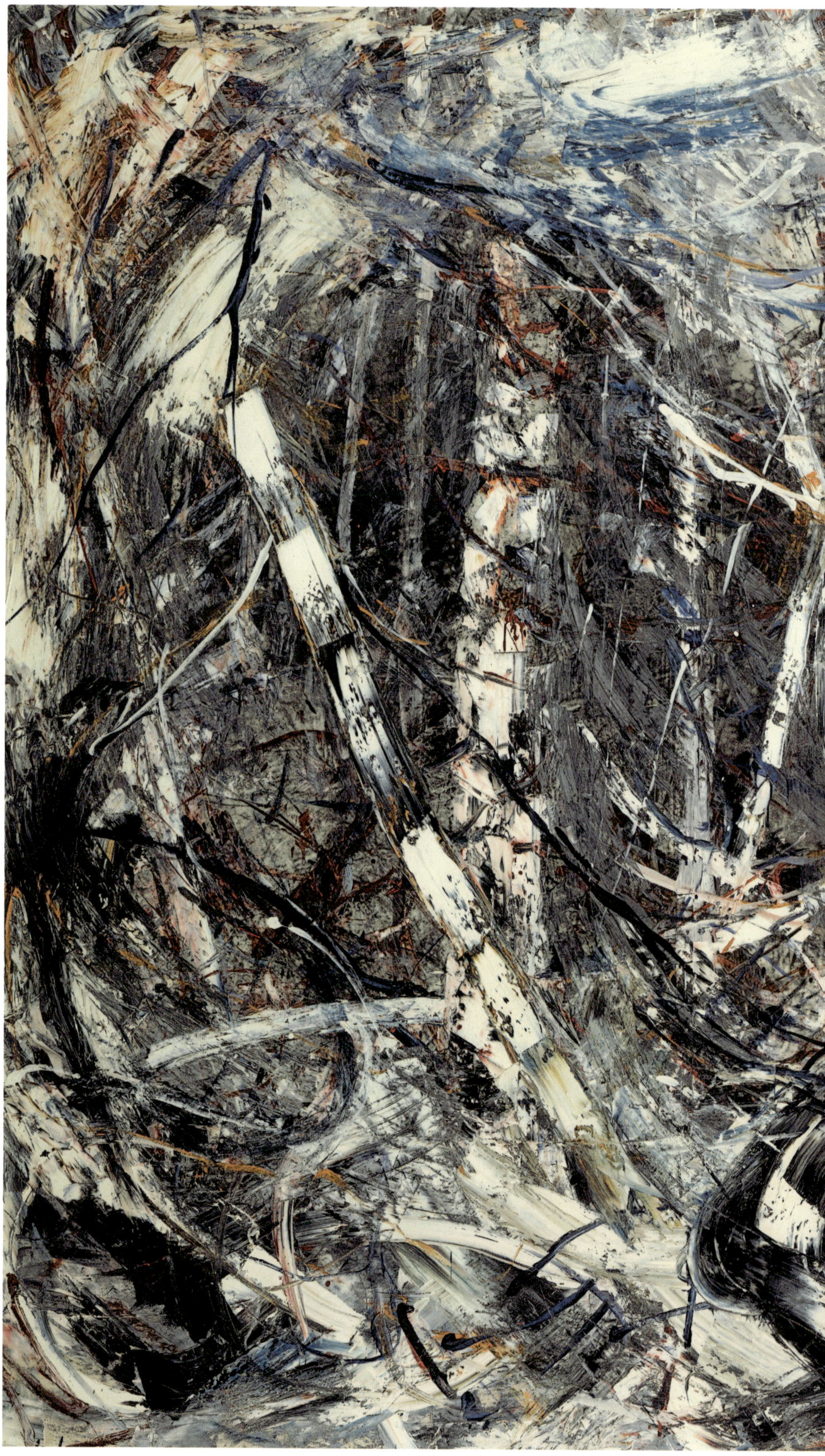

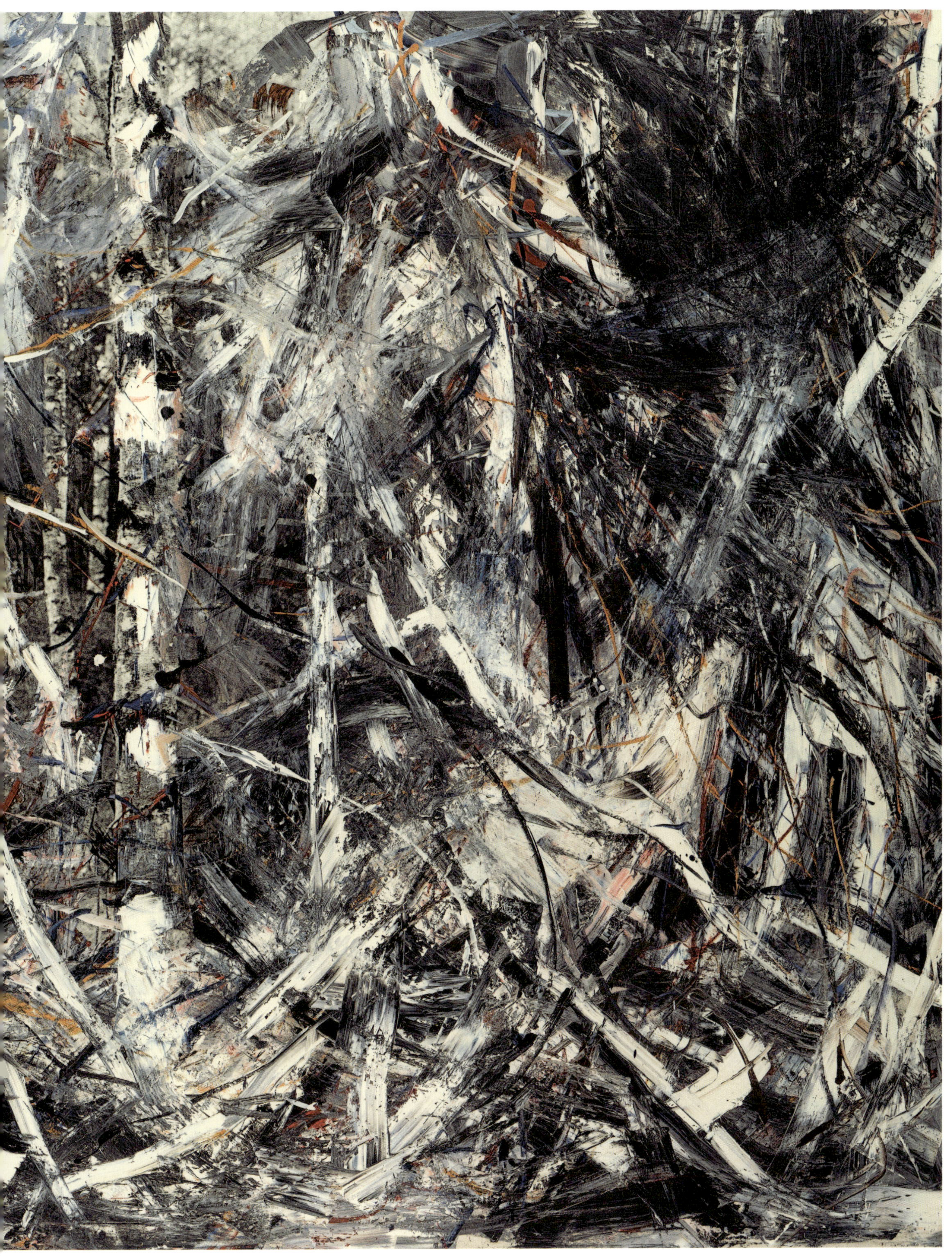

The axis between a constellation of discrete elements (in the 'Sand and Sea' series) and the single, painterly entity of a 'Traditional Landscape' is that of the gradual arrival at the possibility of producing a painting from an early-conceptual departure point which rejected such a solution. It is a trajectory that reinvents a painting's justification for existing through an empirical process of trial and error, without recourse to any of the predetermined cultural parameters according to which painting is the default artistic medium, and a painting the original art object. McKeever could only bring himself to commit to painting by reinventing its wheel. He approaches the medium as though asking, 'What can painting be?', rather than 'What can I make with painting?'

Paradoxically enough, the empirical pursuit of a new justification and means for producing a work of art is consistent with the spirit of early conceptual art, and its determination to recreate the premises and procedures of art-making from scratch, which, in its case, meant the rejection of painting and photography's replacement of it as the primary artistic means of producing an image. The self-reflexivity of McKeever's painterly process is also consistent with conceptualist methods. By offsetting gestural abstract painting with a photographic ground, painting's fundamental properties are rhetorically highlighted. The medium becomes both an instance of itself and a sign for itself. What is being signified is painting's material presence, as distinct from the photograph's record. The effect of this contrast is to spring a temporal schism between the two media in which the familiar presentness of photographic illusion – one of its defining qualities – is pushed into retrospection by the materiality of painting. By contrast, McKeever's application denotes the photographic image, mechanical and reproductive, as innately retrospective and second-hand.

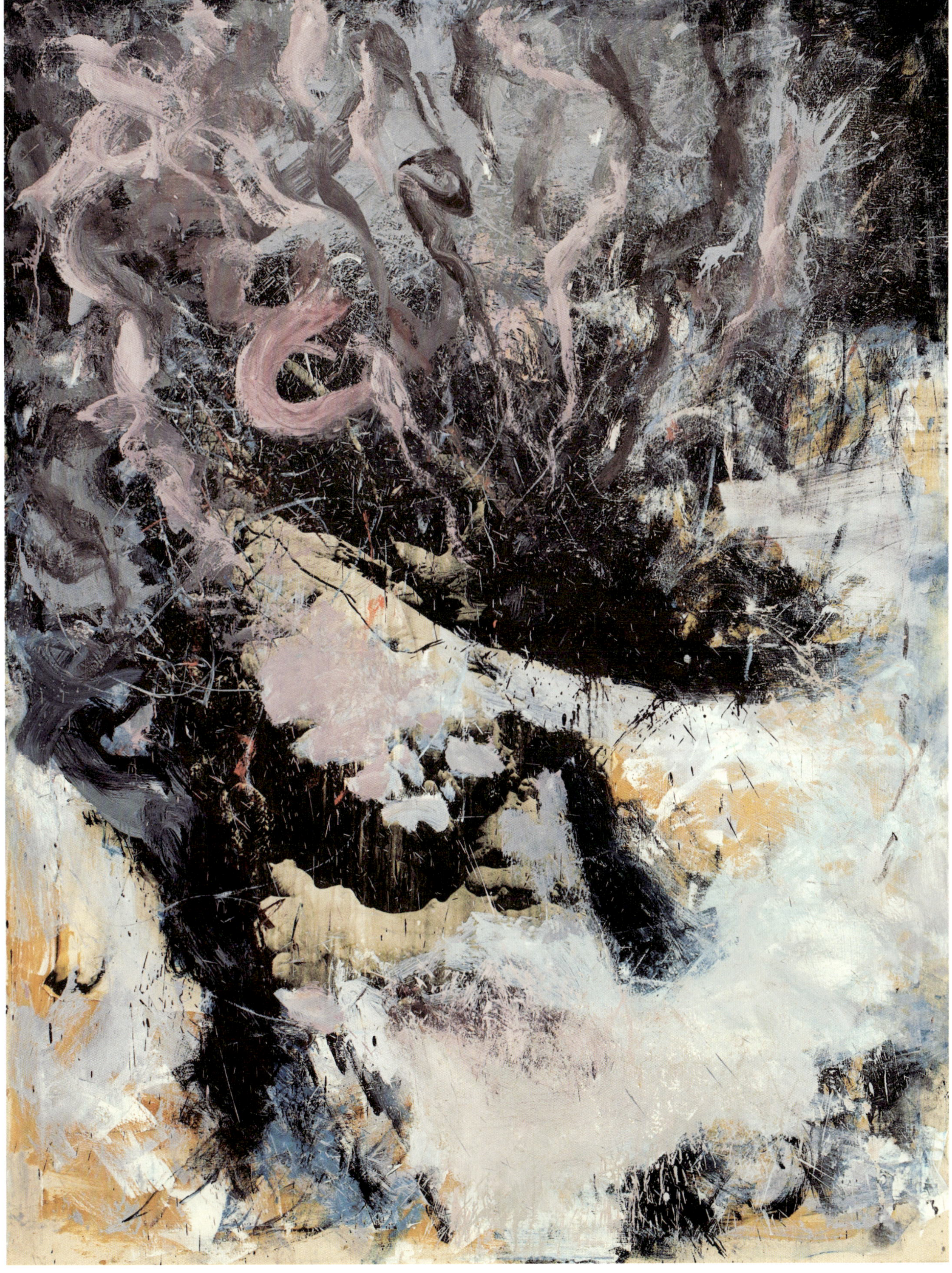

Beside the Brambled Ditch (1983) is painted almost entirely in black and white. Broad sweeps of each colour mix on the surface of a large photograph. Brushstrokes step off into an image of concentric ripples on the surface of a pool. The photograph's illusionistic depth jabs holes in the painterly texture. An image which might be the essence of the brimming present tense is qualified by paint which superficially resembles its monochrome tonalities but possesses an overt, physical substantiality which qualifies the photographic image as definitively past. The vein of emotive nostalgia the 'Traditional Landscapes' are able to access is accounted for by this confining of a photograph's presentness to its evidential claim of 'that-has-been'[10], as much as by their accessing of a historical tradition of landscape representation.

McKeever's title for the series is richly allusive. In conjunction with the English poetic quotes which title many of the individual works, it recalls T.S Eliot's meditation on the value of artistic tradition, in his essay *Tradition and the Individual Talent* (1917), as well as modern poetry which knowingly adopts traditional idioms, such as the strict sonnet forms of Geoffrey Hill's *Tenebrae* (1979). Eliot's proposition of a two-way dynamic between a new work of art and the tradition out of which it arises is congruent with McKeever's dialectical qualification of an archetypal pictorial ground which itself qualifies his actions: 'The existing order is complete before the new work arrives; for order to persist after the supervention of novelty, the whole existing order must be, if ever so slightly, altered; and so the relations, proportions, values of each work of art towards the whole are readjusted; and this is conformity between the old and the new.'[11]

Left exposed to an extent unusual in the series, the photographic ground of *Early Morning – The Needles* (1983) produces a powerful illusion of spatial recession. A rocky

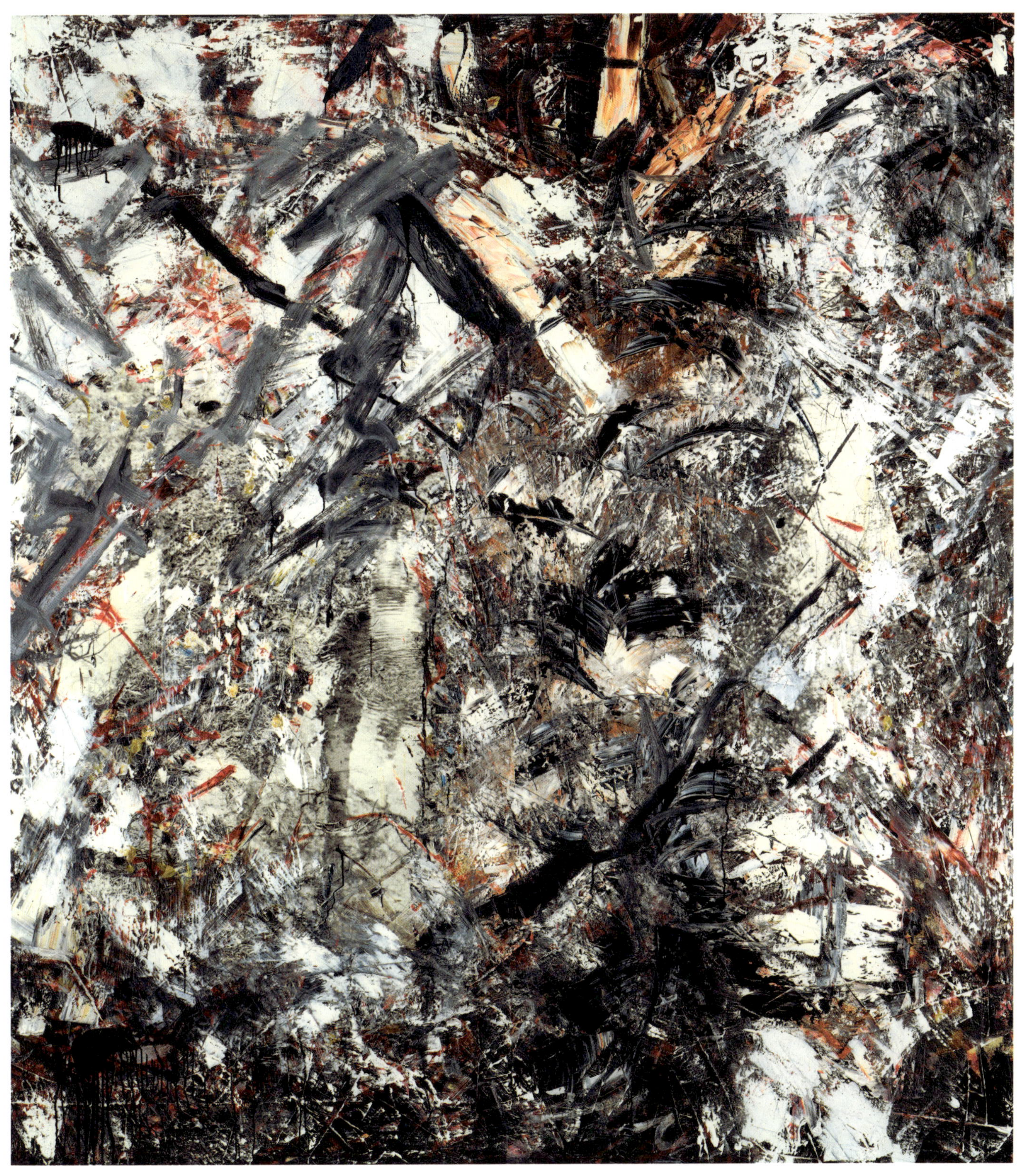

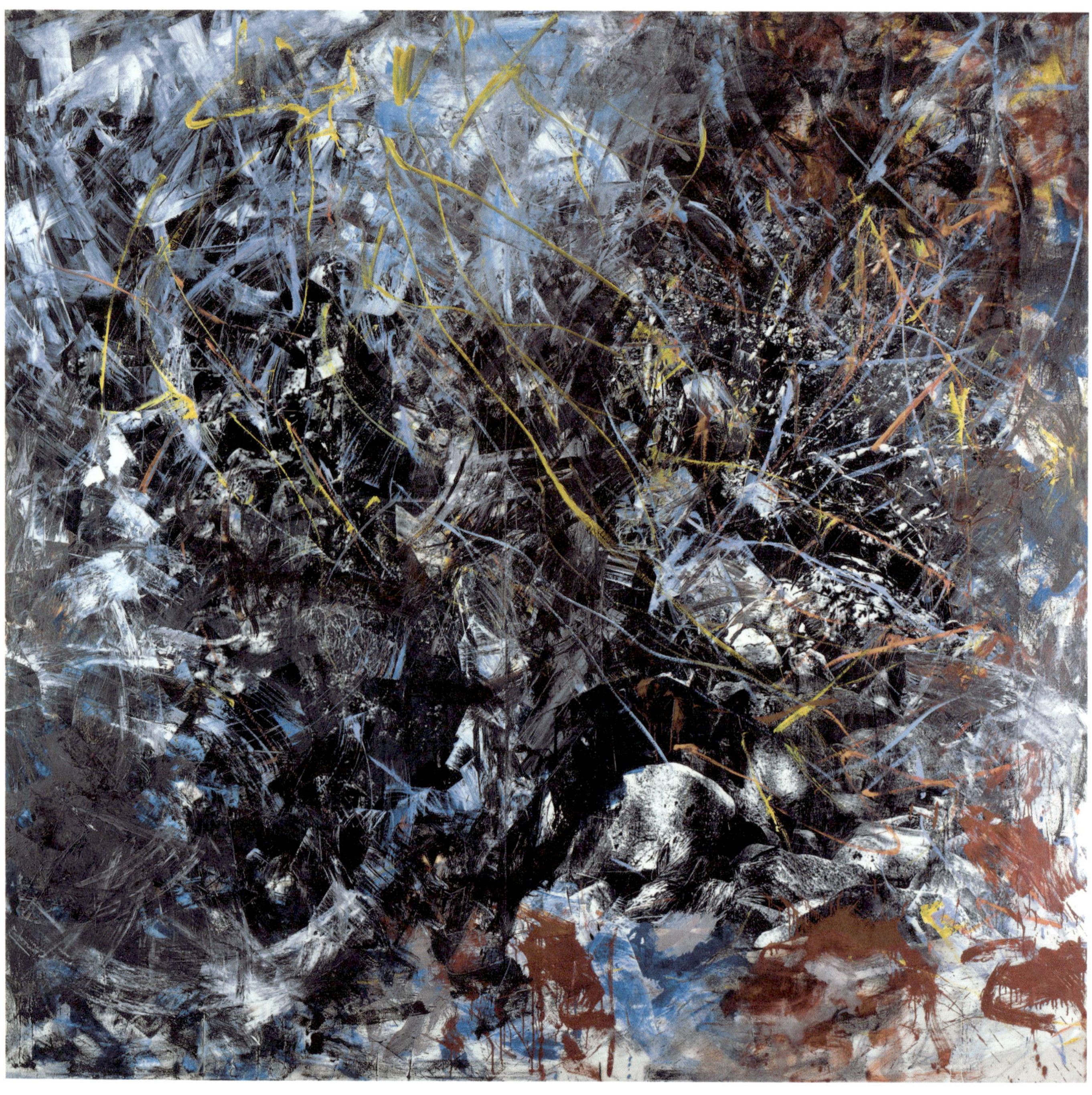

foreground recedes to the foot of a mountain range, its distant peaks dramatically silhouetted by the rising light of dawn. Although this is a black-and-white photograph it might be the sublime image of a 19th century Romantic landscape painting by Caspar David Friedrich. The retrospectiveness of the photographic medium acquires a further, historical dimension as an image of a traditional painterly archetype. By dialectical contrast, painting's qualification of this ground is 'the supervention of novelty', signalled by colour – pale cobalt blues, crimsons, and ochres – brushed wet-into-wet, through thick, white impasto; and by a vigorously gestural method, that rejects technical niceties.

In the 'Traditional Landscapes' series, the gesturalism of McKeever's painterly application is accentuated in order to dramatically distinguish it as the human antithesis of the mechanical, photographic ground. But a consequence of this heightened physicality is that these are the paintings of McKeever in which his mark-making most conforms to the assertion of the painted mark as a form of personal signature. For McKeever, such a reading inclines painting to be interpreted as self-expression in the negative sense in which Eliot defined it: 'Poetry is not a turning loose of emotion, but an escape from emotion; it is not an expression of personality but an escape from personality.'[12] McKeever's problem was to make painterly gesture function as the inverse of a photograph's mechanical image, and yet have it remain impersonal and disinterested enough to register as a credibly objective commentary on the photograph it qualifies.

A striving to expunge painting-as-signature from his application characterises McKeever's transition to the 'Lapland' series (1985–86), which otherwise follows the technical template established by the 'Traditional Landscapes'. All but one of the twenty 'Lapland' works conform to a vertical

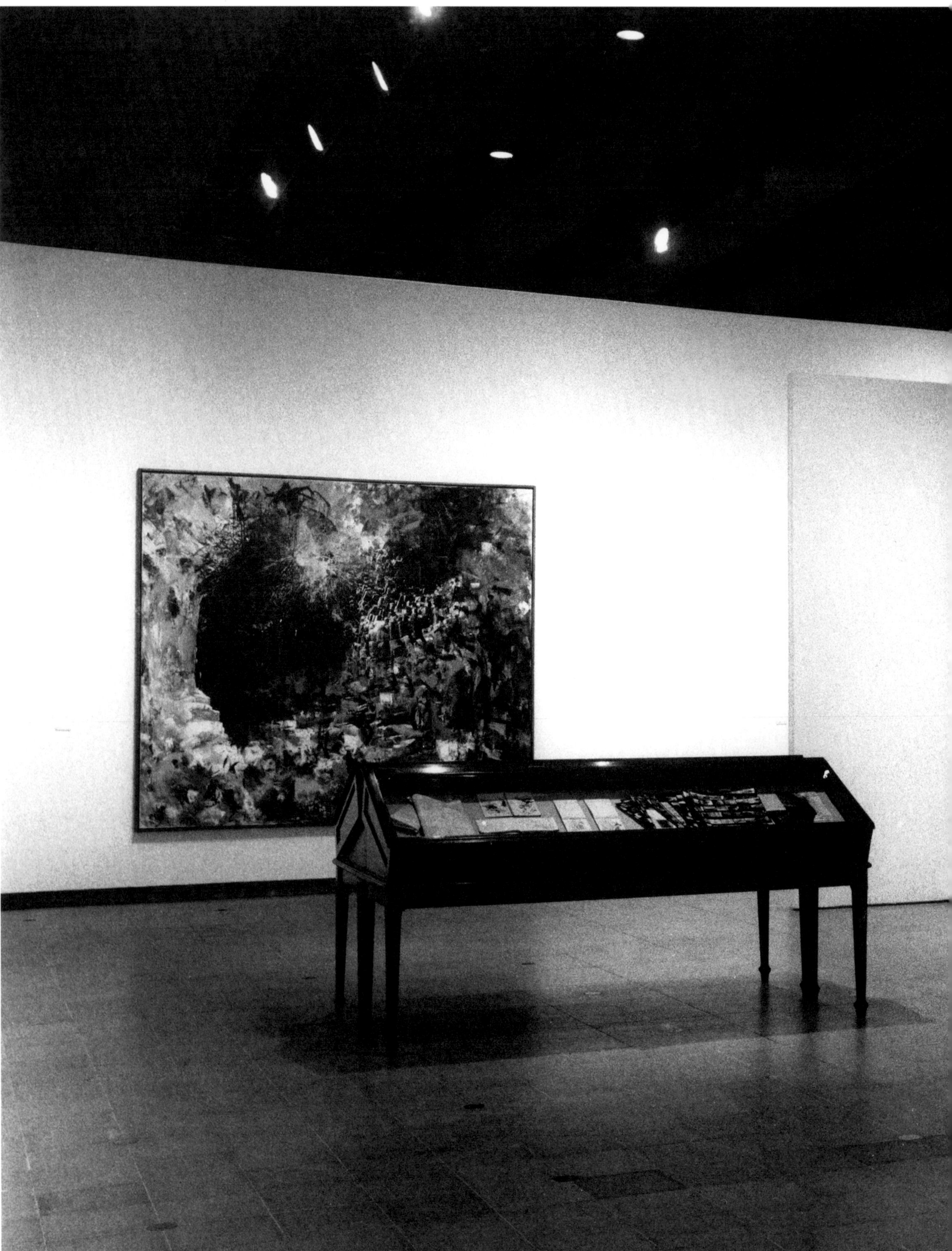

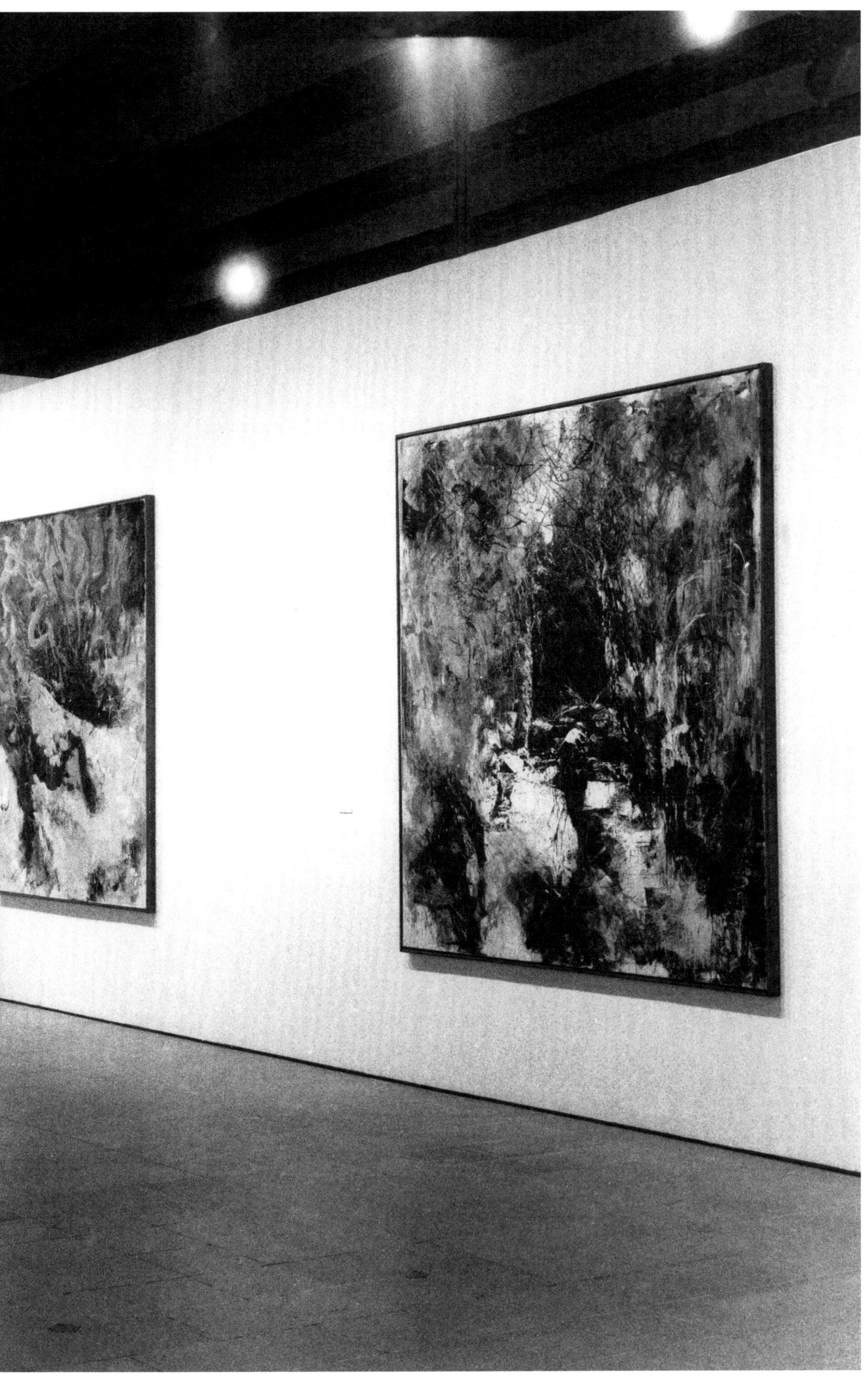

A Journey Through
Contemporary Art
with Nigel Greenwood,
Hayward Annual 1985,
Hayward Gallery,
London

220×170cm format. Whereas the photographic grounds of the 'Traditional Landscapes' are mostly submerged under a thrash of gestural brushstrokes, the 'Lapland' works feature cut-out photographic areas left largely free of paint. The cut-out's unevenly serrated edges operate as a formalistic element within a composition: an abstract drawing defining a juncture between the photographic image and the raw, cotton-duck ground. In *Hearing You Breathe II* (1986), McKeever activates the transition between these areas, exploiting an ambiguity between the curve of a black brushstroke and the fork of a tree's branch, as though photographic illusion were being dragged by his brush from its proper, photographic domain onto the bare canvas. The photographic cut-out of a thicket of branches and foliage which occupies most of the left side of the painting functions as an abstract, biomorphic form in the overall composition. Surrounded by pale stains of oil thinned to seep into the raw fabric, the collaged photograph conversely occupies the materialistic side of a binary which the 'Traditional Landscapes' assigned to impastoed oil paint. Only where McKeever has dynamically extended the dark line of a photographed branch with a swathe of gestural black oil paint do we have the sense of painting being superimposed onto a photograph, rather than vice-versa.

Introducing a technique of staining raw canvas with washes of thinned oil paint enabled McKeever to articulate an impersonal painterly gesture, less directly connoting the hand that applied it. There is a metaphorical relation between the flow of natural activity in the landscape which the photographs represent – river water coursing through a ravine, or the choatic, but rhythmic growth of a tree's boughs – and the seep of paint through absorbent fabric, relatively unimpeded by the painter's hand, except as the catalyst triggering a process. Emulating the appearance of a natural phenomenon, uninfluenced by human intention, the facture of a painting is liberated from a resemblance to Abstract Expressionist action painting, a resemblance which was also cultivated in the 'Traditional Landscapes' in order to develop a dialogue between pre-existing models of painterly abstraction and McKeever's qualification of them.

The 'Traditional Landscapes' are commentaries on the tradition of 20th-century abstract painting as much as on the history of artistic landscape representation. This explicit allusiveness makes the series an isolated occurrence in McKeever's oeuvre which otherwise avoids the explicit references to art of the past which became a defining tendency of British art of the 2000s, such as that of Mark Leckey or Martin Boyce. This archly referential art extends the meaning of 'traditional' from Eliot's definition of a work of art's dynamic relation to its historical context to a generating of

artistic content out of specific references to particular works of art. The historical overview asked of the viewer colludes with that assumed by the artist. Both are sanctioned by access to the established value of a cultural canon that is confirmed by a consensus which at least begins with artist and viewer.

Although the 'Traditional Landscapes' allude to the history of artistic landscape representation, McKeever's empirical process rejects the postmodernist model of art as a sum of constituent references, newly configured. According to such terms, his work would be considered naively predicated on its self-invention through an empirical methodology, and on a conception of the artist's agency transcending that of a floating node, synthesising threads of inherited culture. Although McKeever's art is 'traditional' in Eliot's sense, it rejects the dissolution of artistic subjectivity posited by post-structuralist theory. The step from the 'Traditional Landscapes' – imbued with a consciousness of the tradition

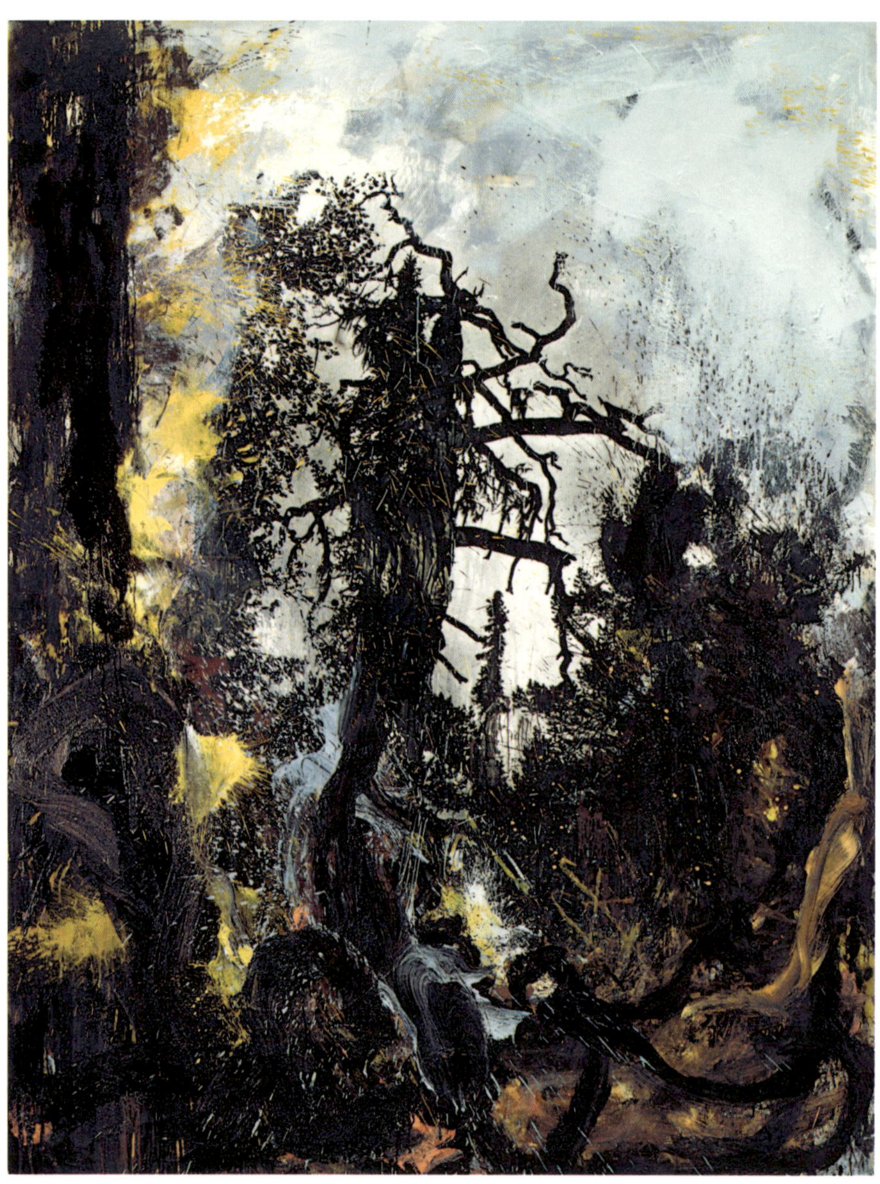

they inherit – to the 'Lapland' series, which allows itself to be shaped by natural processes such as seepage and staining, is also a step further along a line that leads from secondary to primary experience.

Glacier III – Lapland (1986) is composed around a high-contrast photograph of rocks flanking a glacial track. McKeever has stained the unsized cotton canvas which surrounds the collaged photograph with golden brown washes, then scraped and rubbed black and white oil paint into the stains. These various modes of application resist our attempts to unravel the painting's integrated texture into constituent brushstrokes. In the upper area of the painting, pale blue oil paint has been spread over dried black, white and ochre. The blue claims the reality of a sky from the photograph's artifice, as the painterly process conjures a metaphor for an existential experience of the landscape that can only be ascertained from a viewing of the photograph alone by an act of concerted imagination:

an experience of cold, of fluctuating light conditions, of perceptual disorientation, of how a body resists and assents to the conditions it encounters while navigating treacherous terrain. The assertion of painting as a more direct vehicle than a photograph for the conveyance of subjective experience has a heroic ring which is tempered by the painting's abstraction. Only their photographs tether the 'Lapland' works to a landscape idiom. As much as the painterly process is pitched as commensurate with the photograph's landscape referent, it ultimately remains self-reflexive, unable to claim the motif outright. This ambiguity is implicitly anti-heroic.

In 1985, McKeever participated in a two-person exhibition at the Arnolfini Gallery in Bristol[13] in which his paintings were presented in conjunction with those of the British figurative painter Frank Auerbach. The pairing cultivated a comparison between their respective uses of processes usually associated

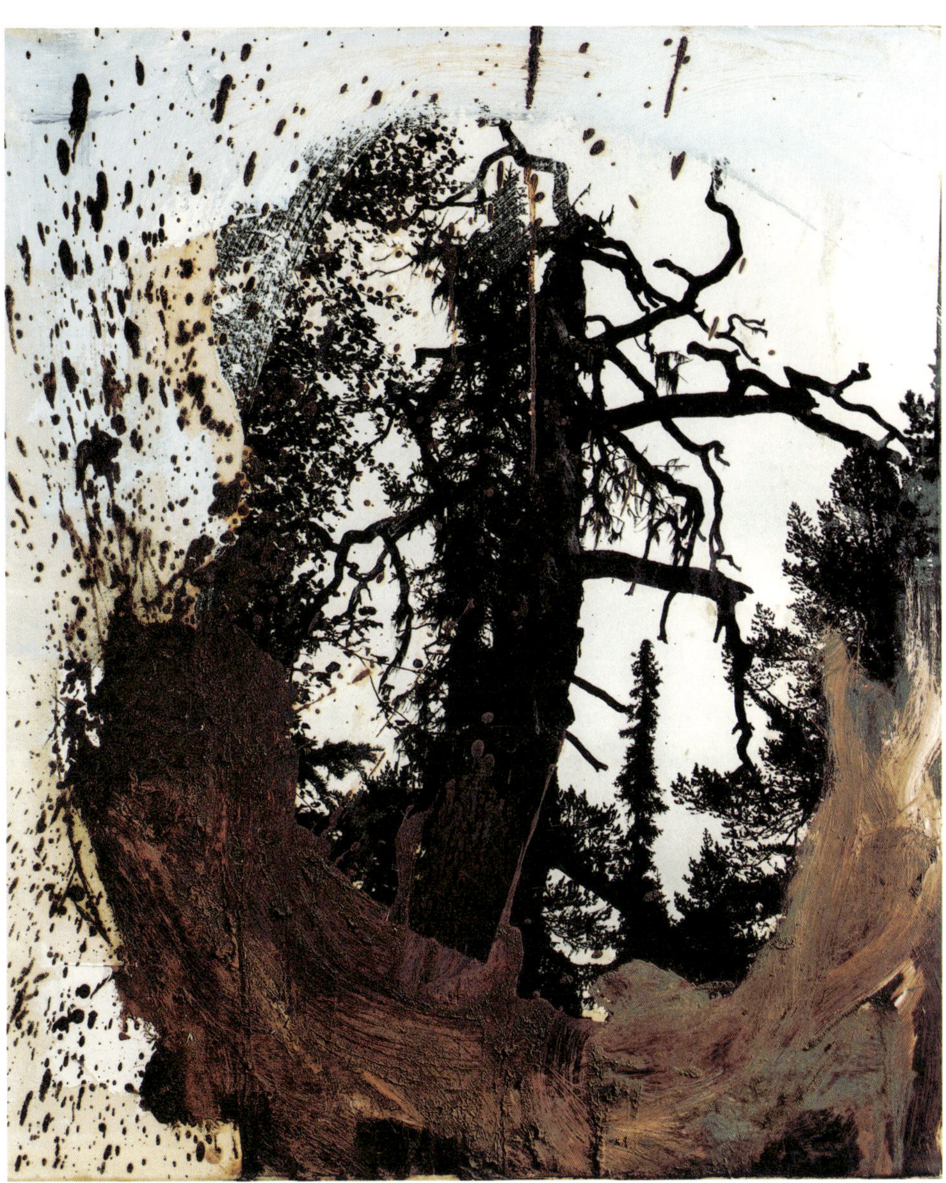

with abstract painting, but to represent nature. In common with the work of Auerbach, and also of Francis Bacon, McKeever's paintings of this period experiment with the potential of combining non-representational mark-making with explicitly representational pictorial information (in McKeever's case, that of the photographic component) in order to evoke sensory experience more vividly than by a traditional, representational language. The abstract means circumvent rational analysis, producing an image less adulterated by habitual preconceptions in order 'to bring the figurative thing up onto the nervous system more violently'[14], in Bacon's words.

In his published interviews with David Sylvester, Bacon explained, 'I don't want to avoid telling a story, but I want very, very much to do the thing that [Paul] Valéry said – to give the sensation without the boredom of its conveyance. And the moment the story enters, the boredom comes upon you.'[15]

He went on to describe the process in detail: 'When I was trying in despair the other day to paint that head of a specific person, I used a very big brush and a great deal of paint and I put it on very, very freely, and I simply didn't know in the end what I was doing, and suddenly this thing clicked, and became exactly like this image I was trying to record.'[16] In Bacon's portraits, non-descriptive mark-making is harnessed to representation – and often the representation of a particular person – by illustrational details which tie non-descriptive marks to their purpose through the association of proximity. In Auerbach's painting, there is no such distinction. Non-descriptive marks seek to realise a paradox: to produce a painted image which is 'like nothing on earth, but like the subject'[17]. The paintings of Bacon and Auerbach implicitly reject photography, except as a source – in Bacon's case – for visual information which would be radically transformed through the act of painting. Bacon sometimes commissioned photographs to be taken of his models for this purpose, but always used them indirectly, as an imaginative cue for a painting process, and never exhibited photographs.

McKeever's photographic grounds perform a role equivalent to the illustrational details in Bacon's portraits; and as in Auerbach's work, McKeever's gestural, non-descriptive marks transcend the limitations of descriptive rep-resentation in order to invoke 'sensation' to which such representation has no access, or one weakened by familiarity. But if McKeever shares with these artists the purpose of finding unfamiliar means of conveying primary experience through painting, he differs in the resolute abstraction of his painting process. Whereas they seek to revitalise figurative painting, only the photographic element ties McKeever's painting to a referent. The 'Lapland' series is a deconstruction of representation rather than a series of landscape representations; and yet it proposes that given the associative trigger of the photograph, non-descriptive paint may evoke sensory and psychological experience more tellingly than representational modes, and therefore indirectly become a form of representation.

The 'Lapland' paintings are simultaneously pictorial, metaphorical, and concrete. Pictorial in their photographic backgrounds, and in the splashes, smears and stains of oil paint which have a partially mimetic relation to landscape phenomenon, such as moving water, branching trees or scudding clouds. Metaphorical in that the gestural dynamism with which McKeever animates paint invokes the dynamic natural processes that animate the landscape, without literally depicting them. Concrete in that the paintings possess a formidable, physical presence which takes the measure of the impact of the natural world on a viewer's senses.

The transition to the 40-panel painting installation *A History of Rocks* (1986-88) and the subsequent series

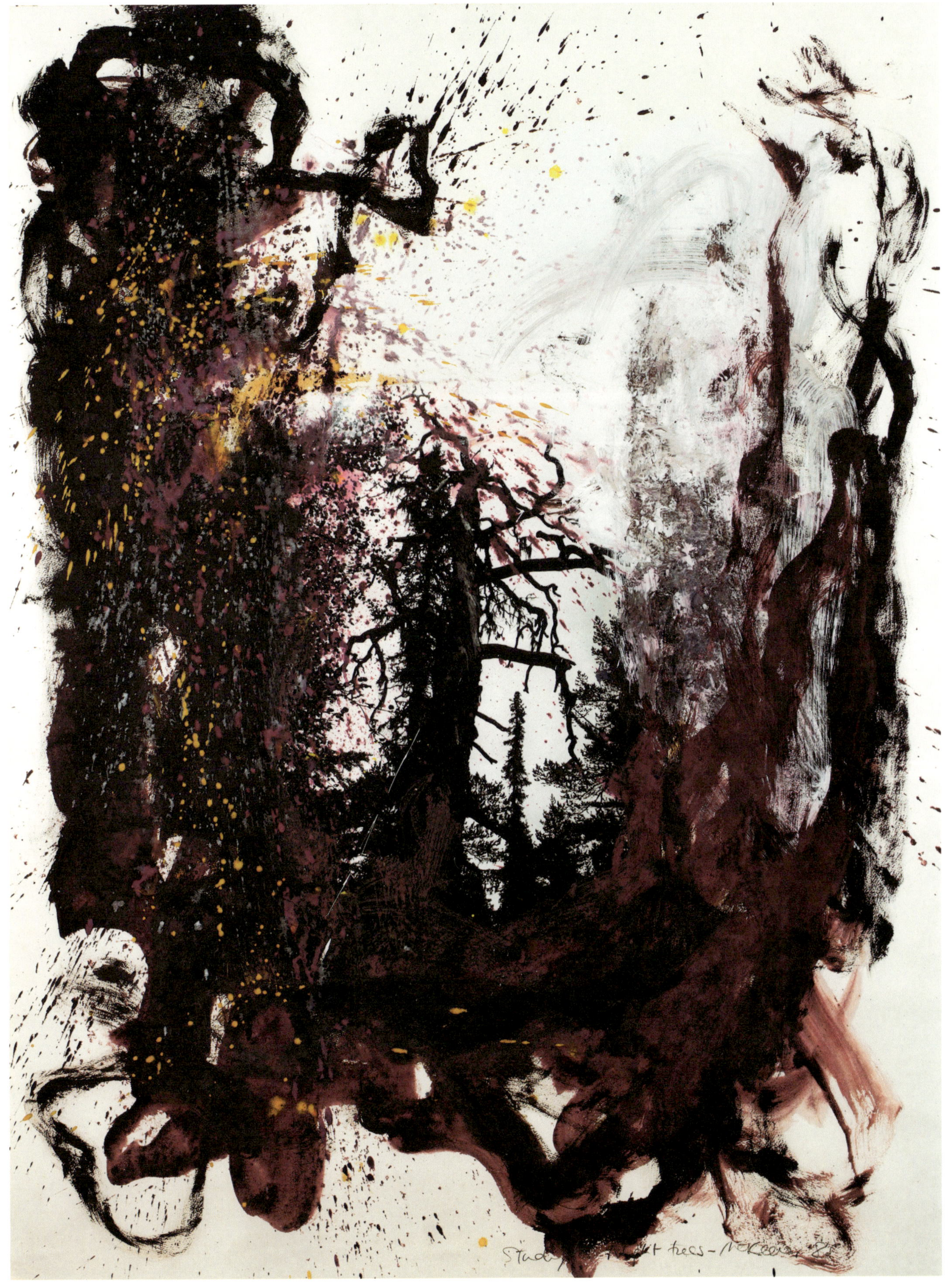

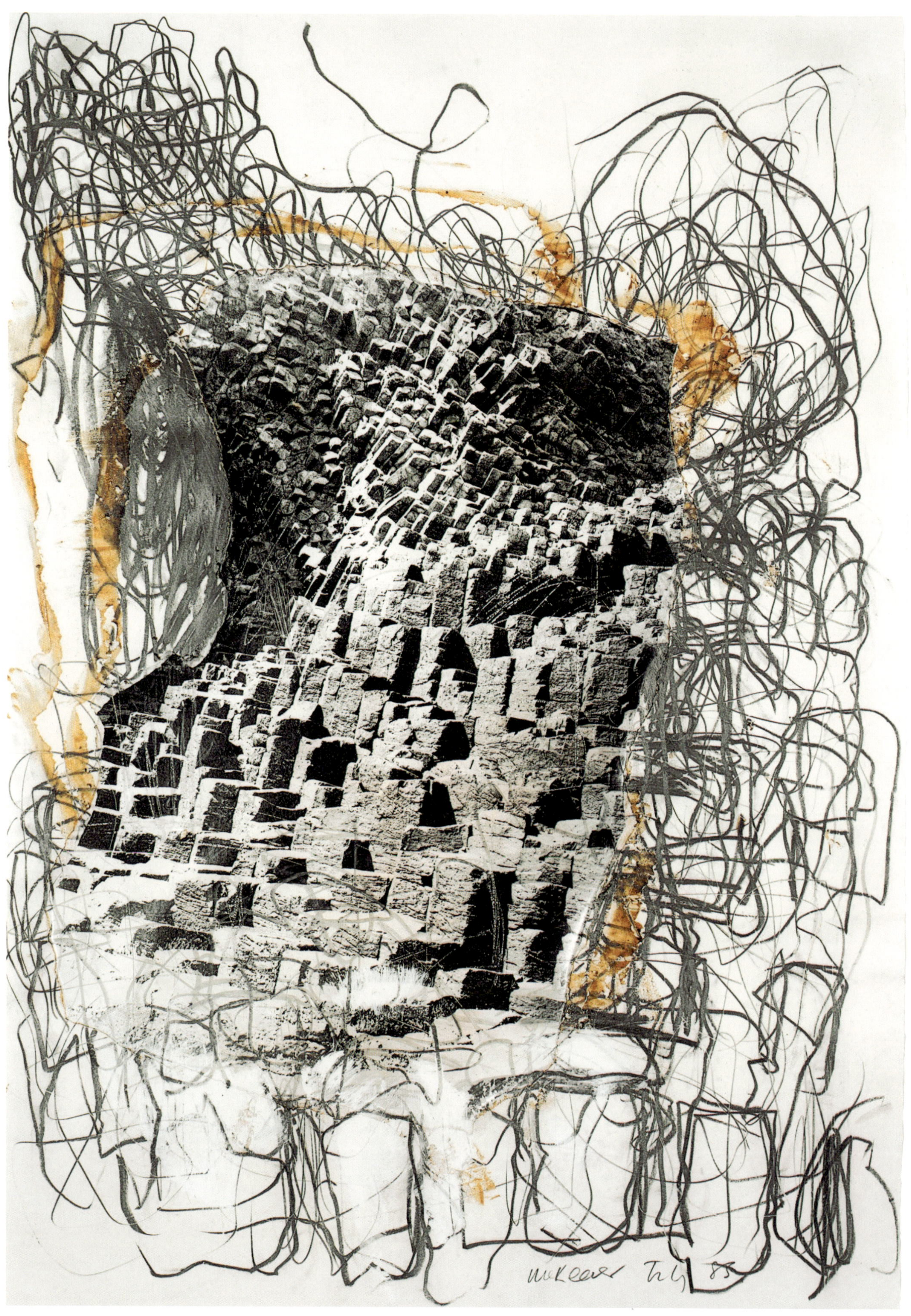

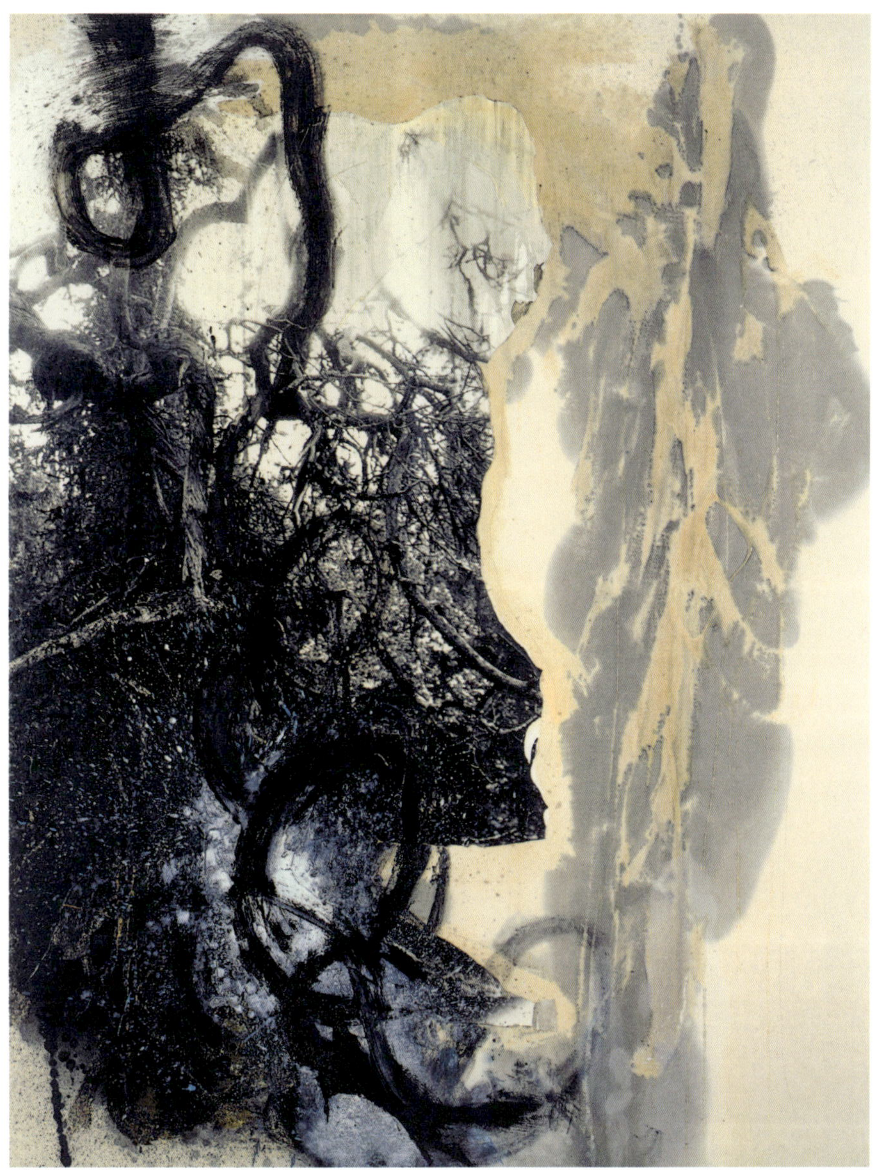

of 'Diptychs' is one of McKeever's recognition that the superimposition of painting onto a photograph may limit painterly abstraction from ranging fluidly across the full range of the possibilities the 'Lapland' series intimates. The photographic element functions like a stage set upon which McKeever's gestural painting 'performs'; and to extend the analogy, a stage has defined parameters. The painting superimposed onto the photograph is confined to the pictorial plane of photographic illusion, and to a dialectical relation by which each medium is perceived as contingent upon the other. McKeever's sidelining of the photographic component in *A History of Rocks* suggests that, in a dialectic between photography and abstract painting, however much painting is cast as the primary qualifying agent that largely obliterates the photograph, photographic legibility will always coerce the greater ambiguities of painterly abstraction to accord with the sense it posits. The painting is accommodated by its

photographic stage, and perceived according to the spatial dictates of its illusionism. This coercion was encouraged by McKeever in the 'Traditional Landscapes' and the 'Lapland' series, but he subsequently resisted its tendentious pull.

As its title hints, *A History of Rocks* is both a summary and retrospective of McKeever's previous development. Its tiled format recalls the gridded structures of early conceptual art which characterised McKeever's work of the mid-1970s, such as the 'Sand and Sea' series, although it dismantles the representational model upon which those structures were based. Like 'Sand and Sea' series, *A History of Rocks* cross-references between disparate types and sources of information. The techniques of seepage and staining which emerged in the 'Lapland' series are extended by the marbling and fracturing of colour. The correspondence between painting process and natural processes, which was a central theme of McKeever's early landscape-sited projects such as *Painting for a Hole in the Ground*, is reiterated. McKeever's reflections, in 1978, on those early, site-specific projects are relevant to the methods he brought to *A History of Rocks*: 'Painting is a natural phenomenon, like snow or rain. It is also a codified activity that has its own sense of time and space.'[18] Taking his cue from the technical advances of the 'Lapland' series, in which the nuanced, tonal ground of a black-and-white photograph or oil-stained canvas would be qualified by gestural painting, McKeever treats canvases heavily-impastoed with black oil paint, or collaged with a photographic fragment, as a surface on which to initiate chemical reactions in which oil paint partially rejects the addition of water-based acrylic. The lack of human influence on the detailing of these events implicitly questions where nature ends and artifice begins.

Installed at the Kunstforum in the Städtische Galerie im Lenbachhaus, Munich, in 1989, the complete work spanned three walls of a large exhibition hall, in two parallel rows of twenty panels – a narrative progression that can be read vertically as well as horizontally. The sequence is almost entirely monochrome, except for brief passages of green, red and brown staining in panels to the far-left and right of the

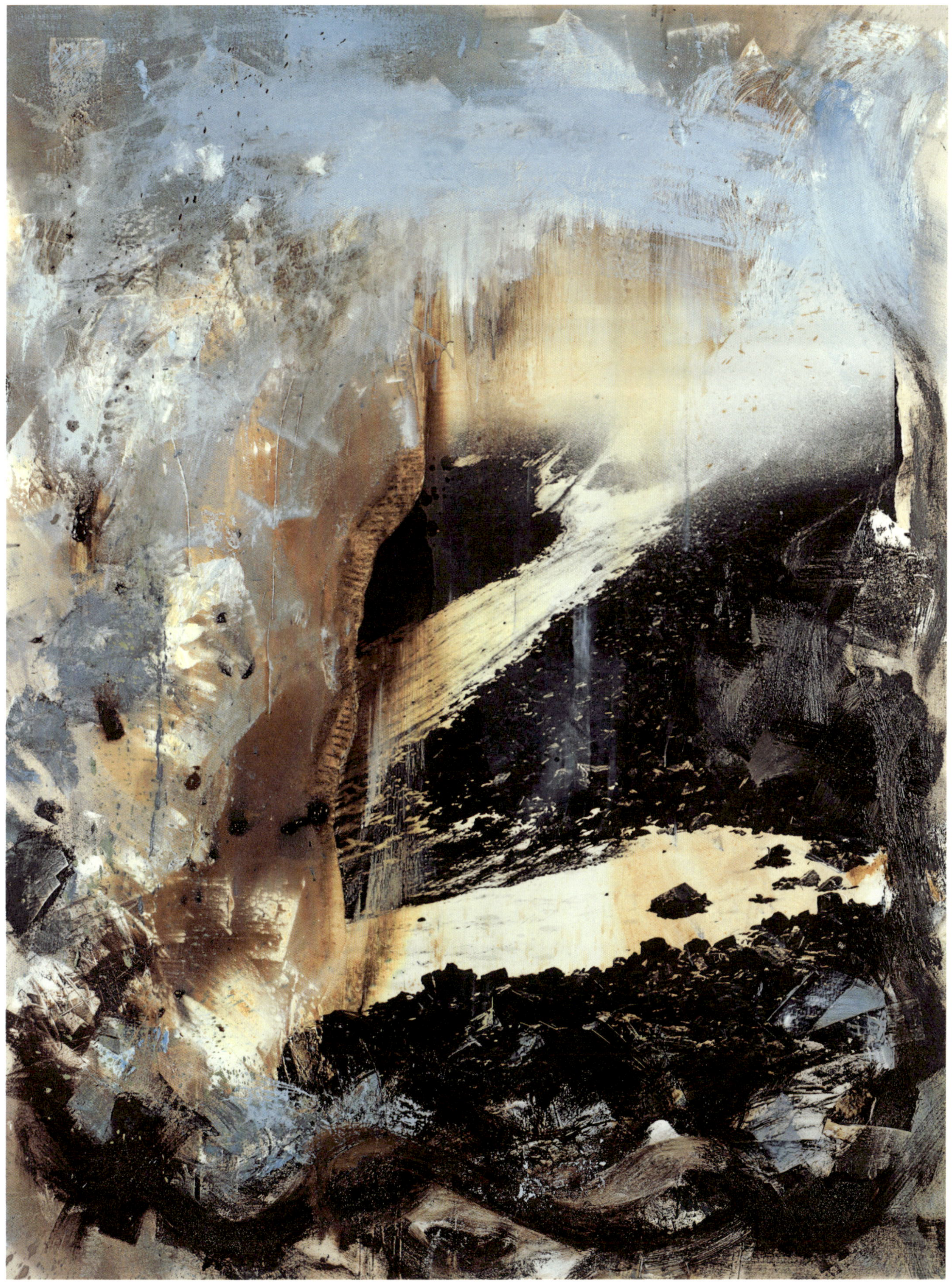

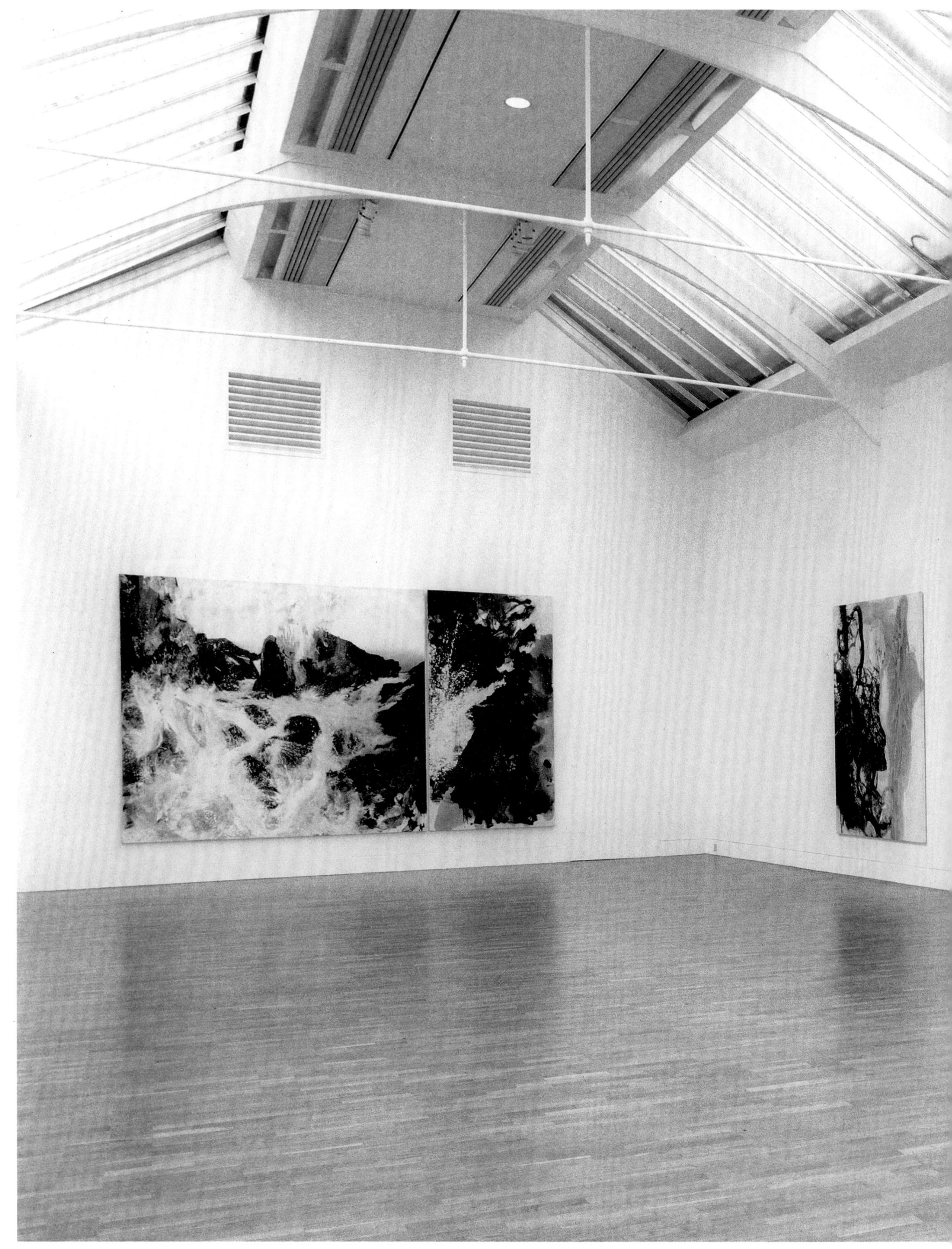

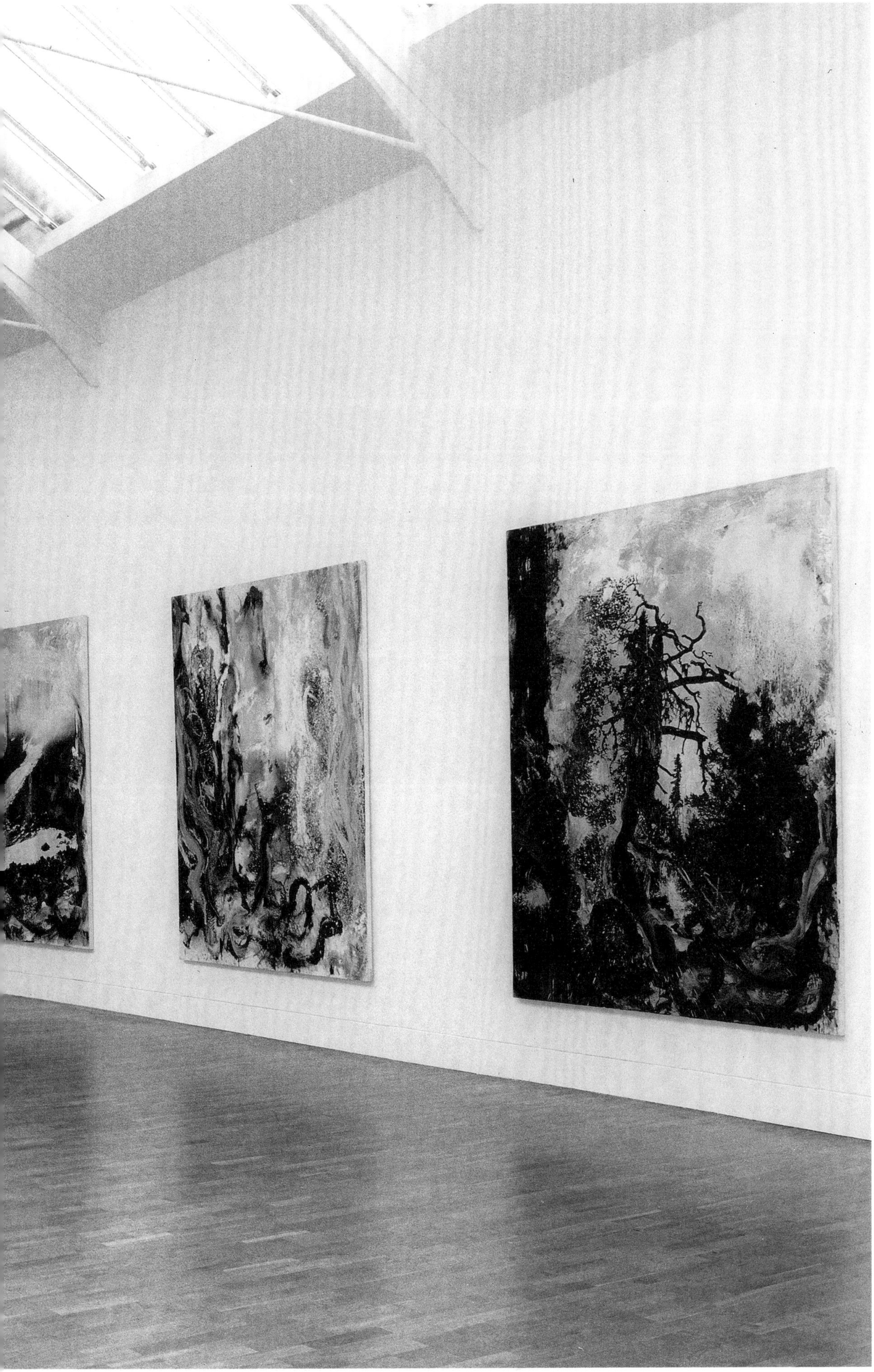

Paintings 1978–1990,
(Lapland Paintings),
Whitechapel Art
Gallery, London , 1990

Landscape study, Scotland, 1982

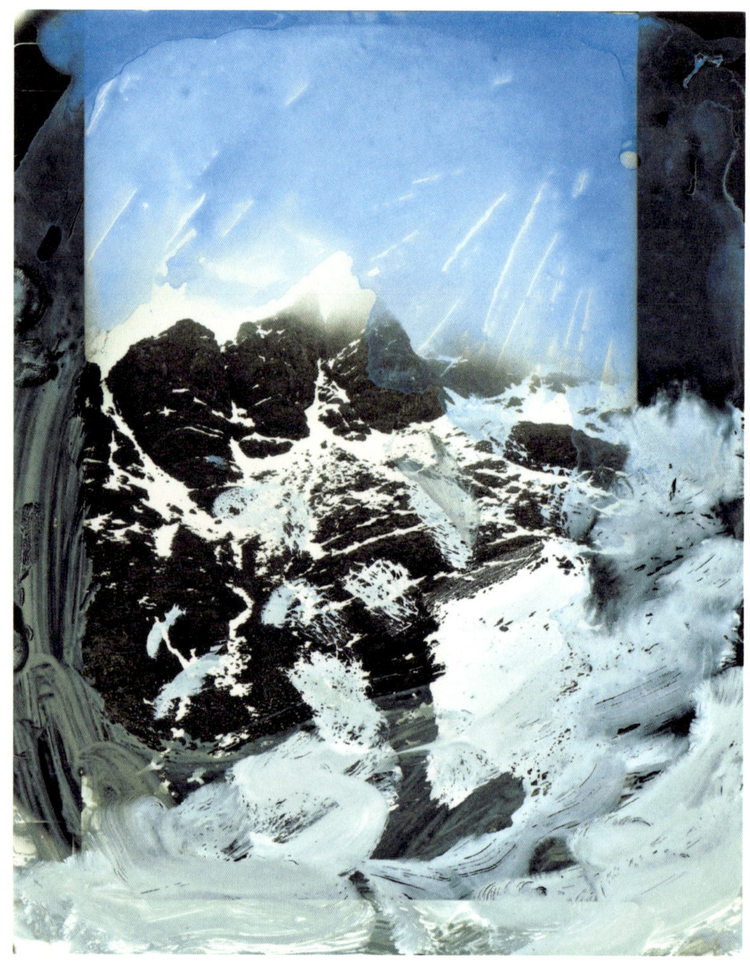

Landscape study, Greenland, 1988

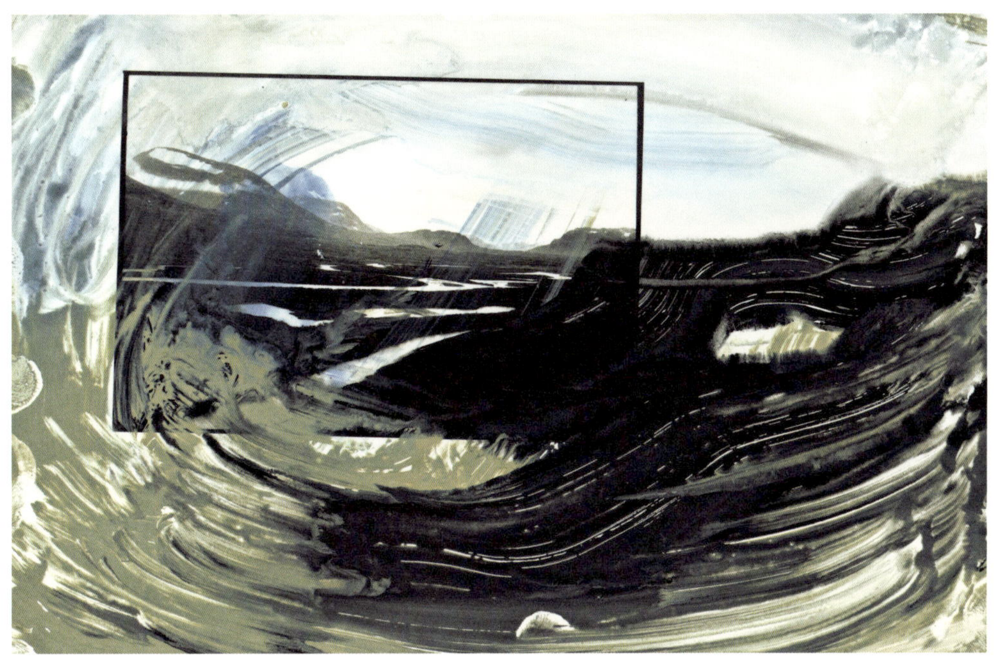

installation. Photographs also appear only at the extremities. Towards the middle of the spectrum, tonal gradations are relinquished to the high contrast of unmixed black and white paint: a white canvas in which a single black cell hovers; or a panel of textured black impasto over which bands of white acrylic splinter and squirm, radiating an aura of droplets. The emphasis of the photographic fragments is directed away from their landscape motifs to the photographic medium itself through the inclusion of the black sprocket holes and frame divisions of the film strip from which they were printed.

Confirming McKeever's structuralistic intent, many of these reproduced frames have been exposed to heat or a chemical agent which has eroded the sprocket edges, and distorted and eroded the images they contain. The viewer's attention defaults from the landscape motif to the mode of representation itself, as if McKeever were intent on effacing any last traces of the romantic ideal of landscape as painting's

'escape valve' from its own materiality, and, by inference, from the urban-rooted viewpoint of post-industrial culture. Michel Foucault's *The Archaeology of Knowledge* (1972) influenced and informed McKeever during the period he was working on *A History of Rocks*. Foucault writes that 'we shall not pass beyond discourse in order to rediscover the forms that it has created and left behind it; we shall remain, or try to remain, at the level of discourse itself'[19]. He intends 'to dispense with things'.[20] It is proposed that to reassess the common patterns discovered within 'discourse', as it trangresses the boundaries of what have been considered autonomous disciplines, is to loosen 'the embrace … of words and things'[21] and therefore, implicitly, of representation.

Multiplicitous, but perceptible in a single, sweeping gaze, *A History of Rocks* atomises the last vestiges of binary structure – whether between photography and painting, or landscape representation and abstraction – that remains in the 'Lapland'

Following spread:
A History of Rocks,
1986–1988.
A work in 40 parts

series. The work's open-ended structure can no longer be paraphrased as a contrast between media or methodologies, and cedes to more ambiguous distinctions: between micro- and macro-scale imagery, or between alternative time signatures. The image of a photographic reel comprehends the retrospective photographic landscape image as well as the click of a camera's shutter followed by another. Linear narrative development, consisting of a series of discrete instants, qualifies the single vignettes which constitute it. Three alternative conceptions of time – that of the pictured landscape, the instant of its being photographed, and a sequence of those instants in a film reel – are combined into a single detail. A canvas painted all black – the colour applied manually in strokes of thick oil paint – is the ground over which tracks of white acrylic trace an alternative conception of time's elapsing, qualifying accretion with simultaneity. Time as substance qualifies time as measure.

The drips of white acrylic follow a single, temporal pulse – McKeever's tipping of the canvas – but they diverge into an array of individual tracks, like the forking of fates that quantum mechanics tells us occurs when an electron is fired through a particle accelerator.

In several of the panels, black oil paint fractures into miniature islands of colour when poured into a pool of white acrylic. This patterning resembles the images of fractal configurations which pictorially represent the order within natural processes, as revealed by chaos theory. Fractals are both an abstraction – graphically signifying data gathered from natural occurrences, such as weather cycles or water flow – and a representation of the symmetry and unpredictability to be discovered in organic structures such as skin cells or snow crystals. McKeever cultivates this ambiguity, challenging us to distinguish a painterly event as image or abstraction. The photographic grounds of the 'Lapland' series define

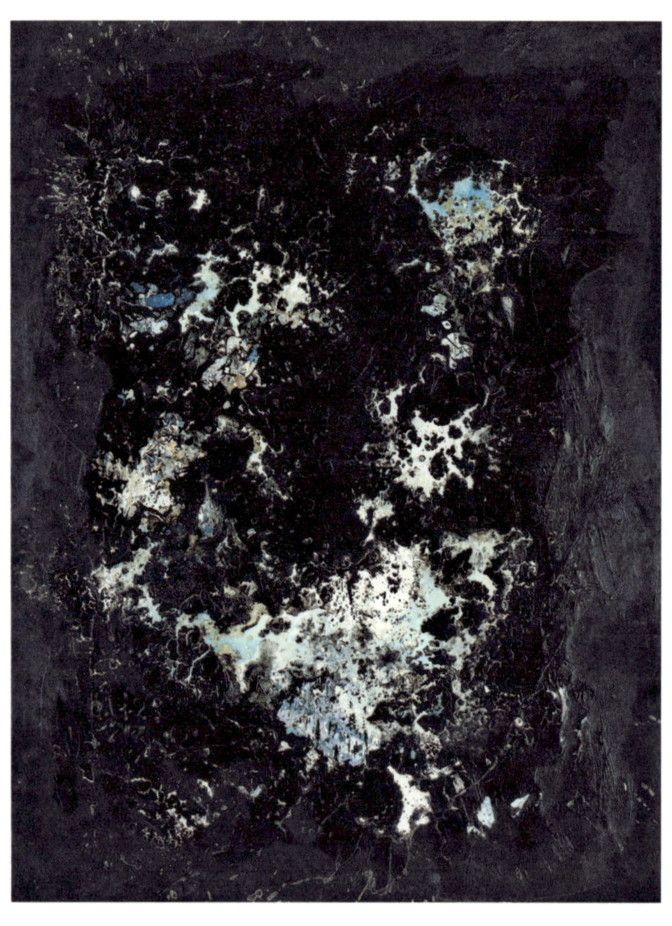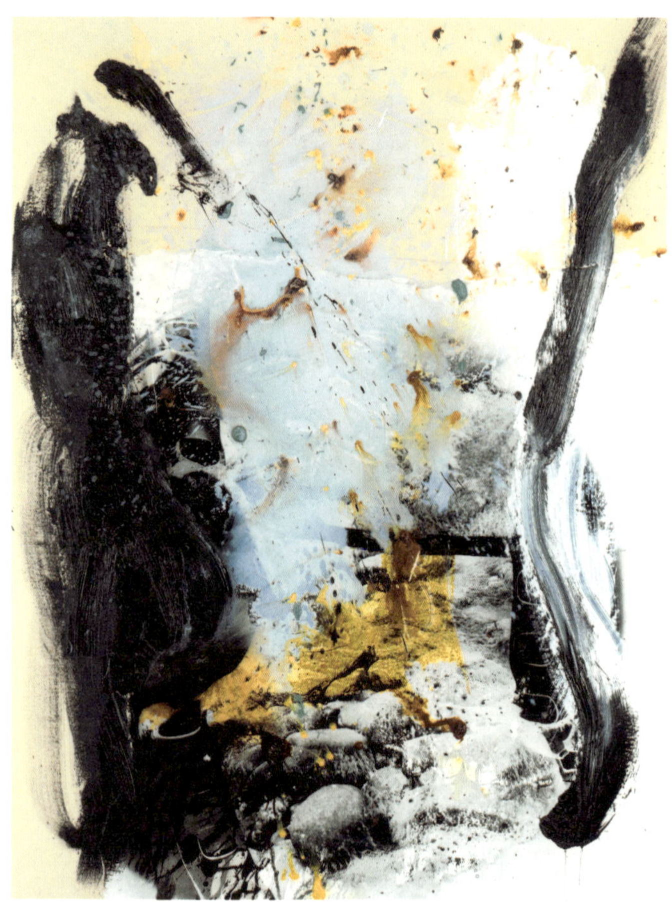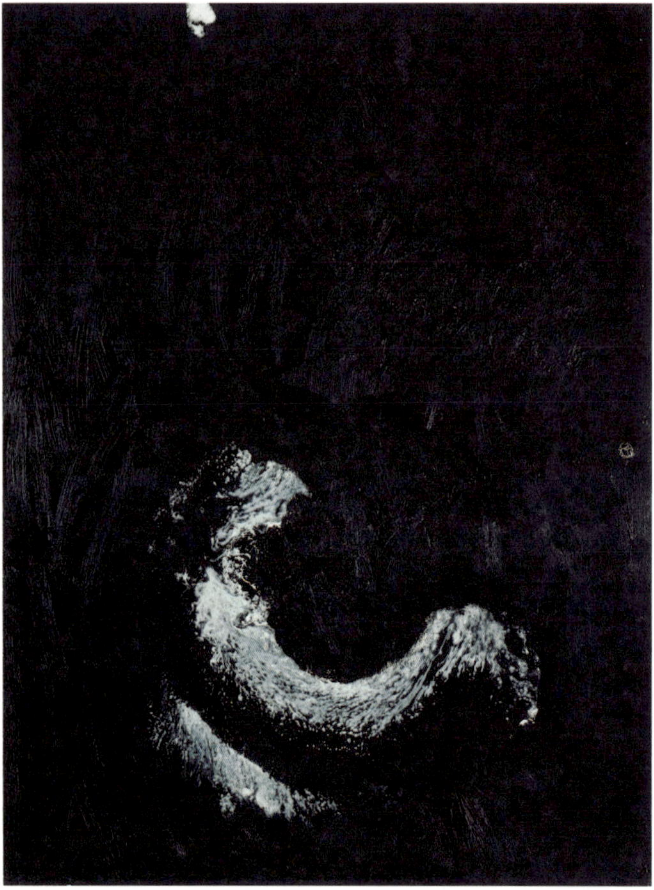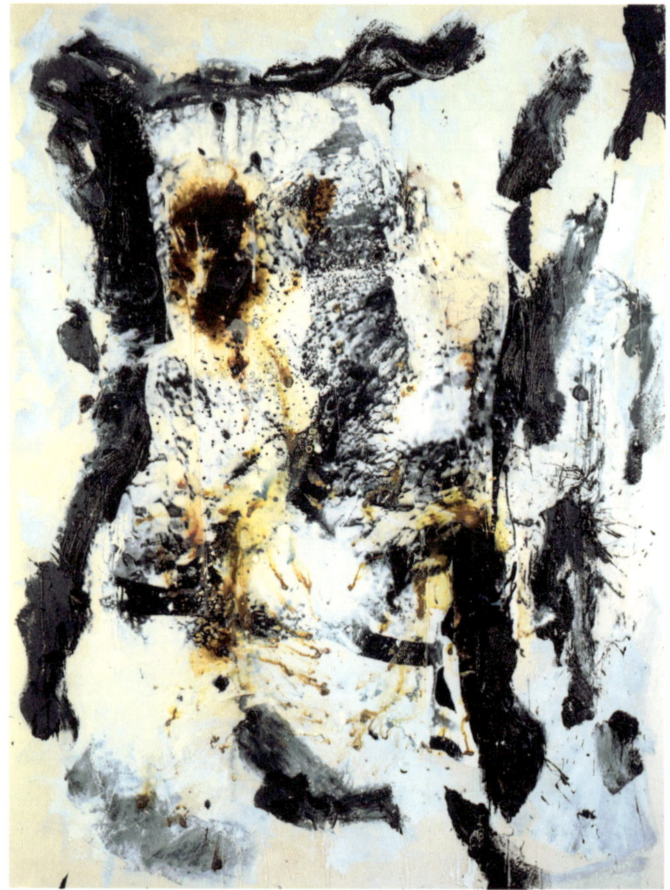

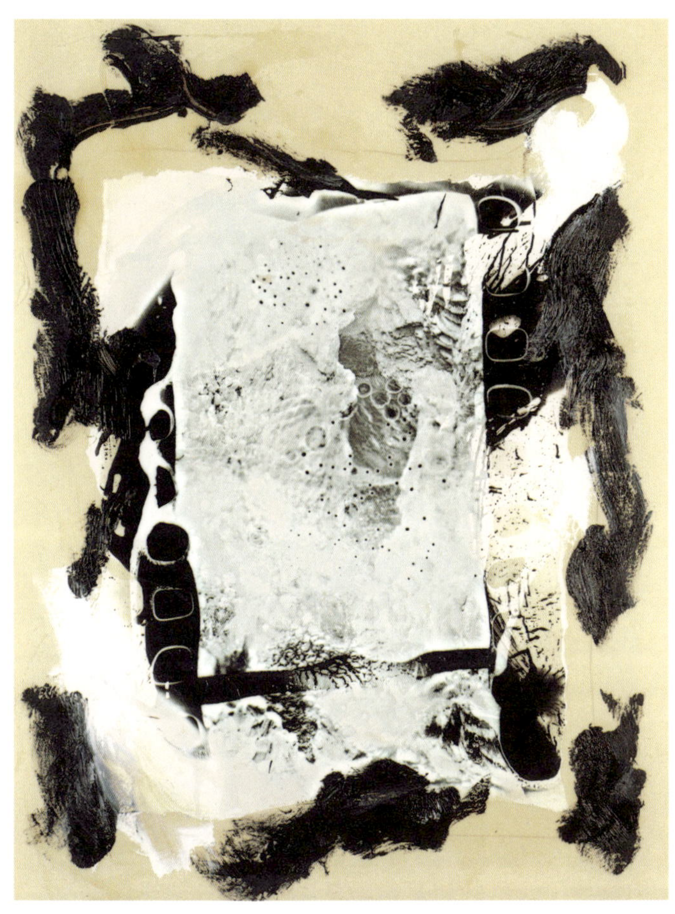
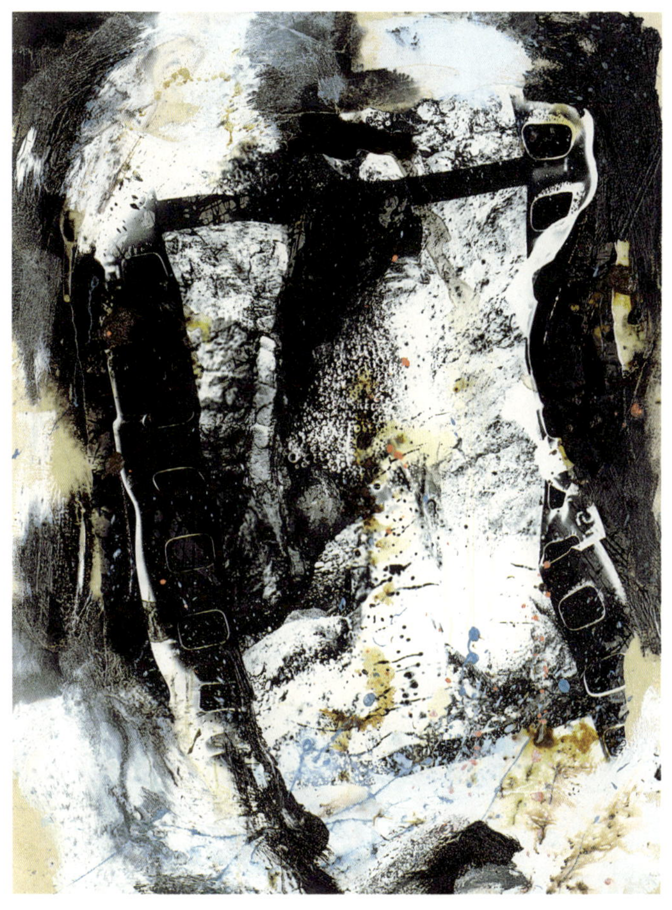
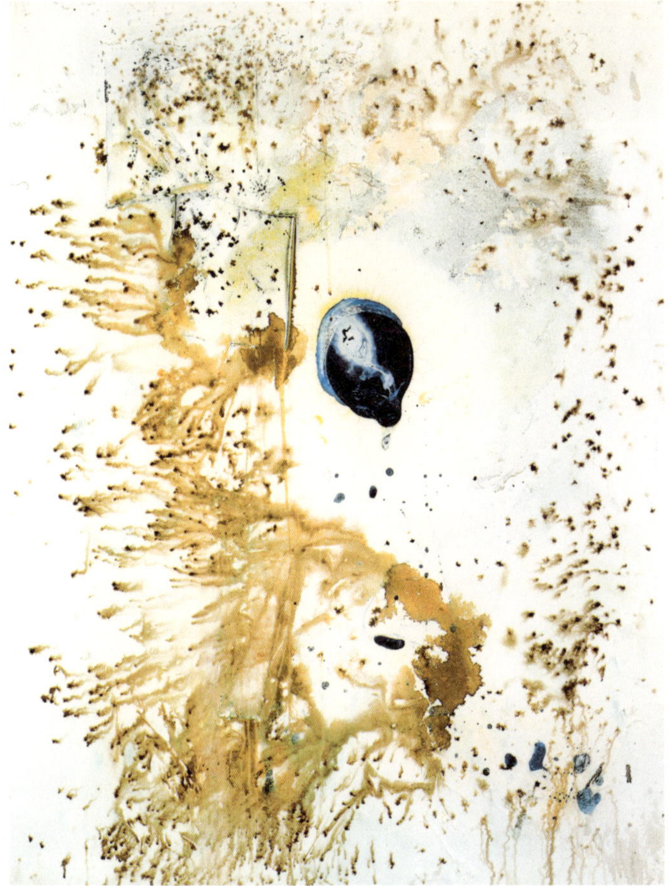
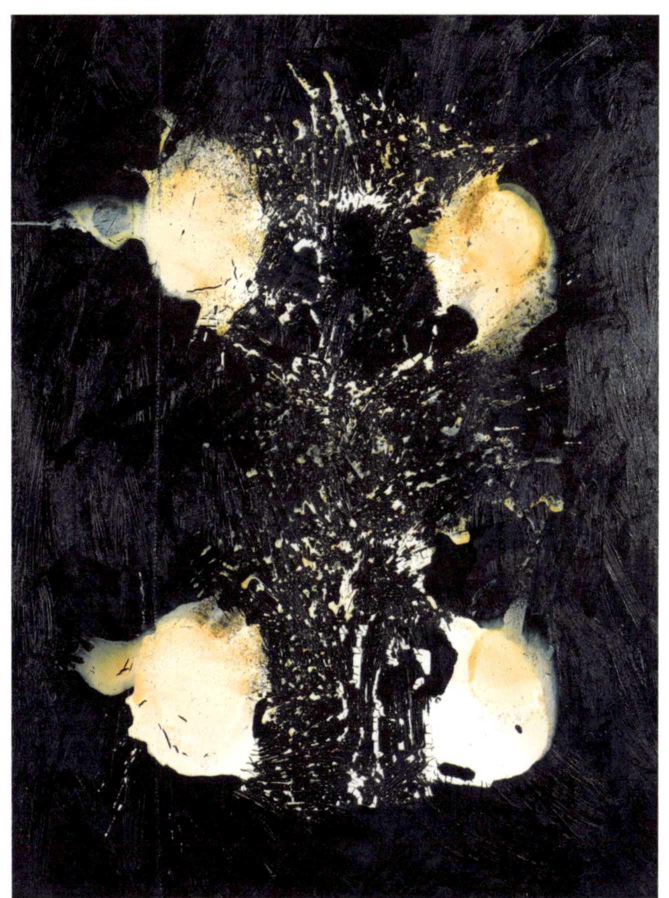

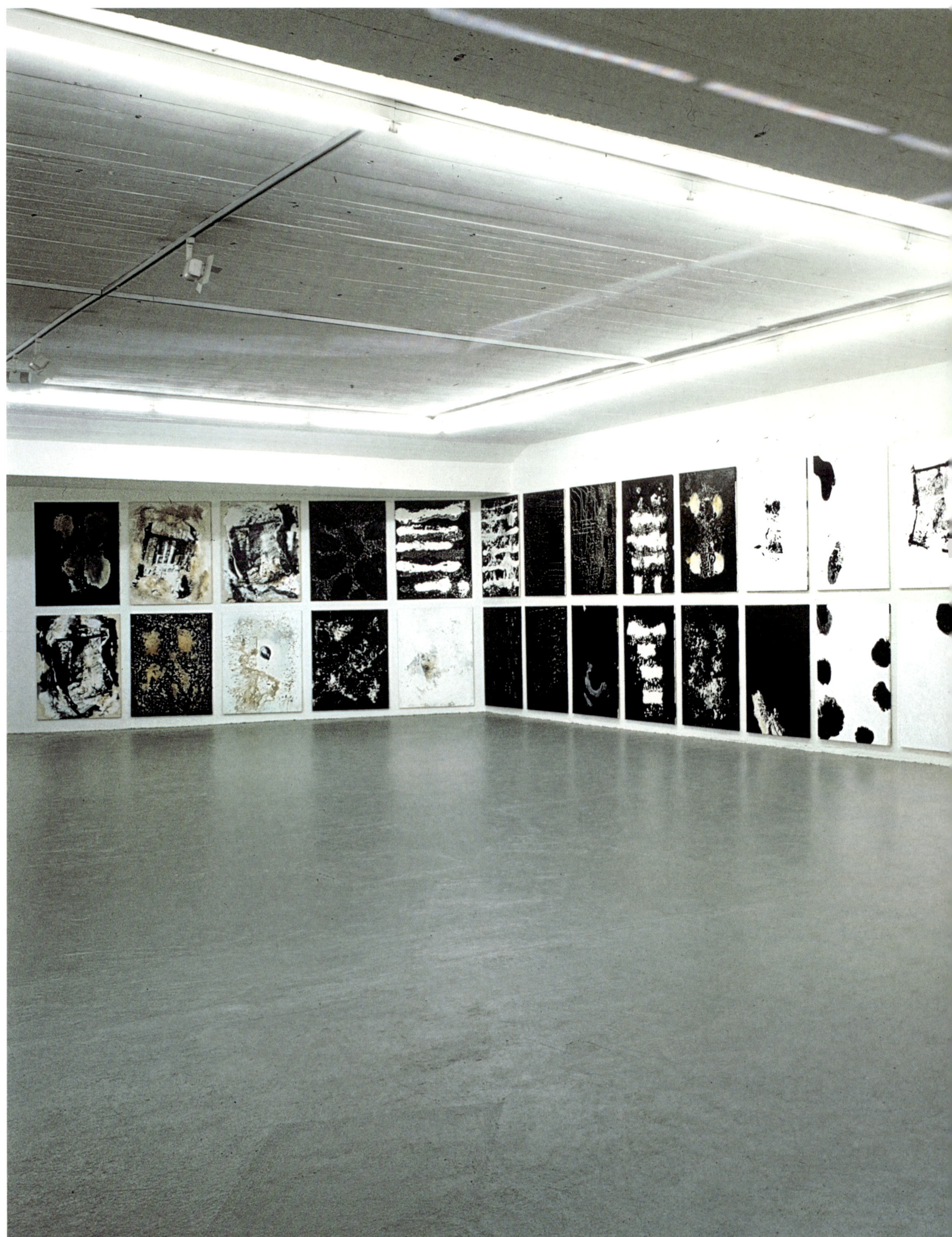

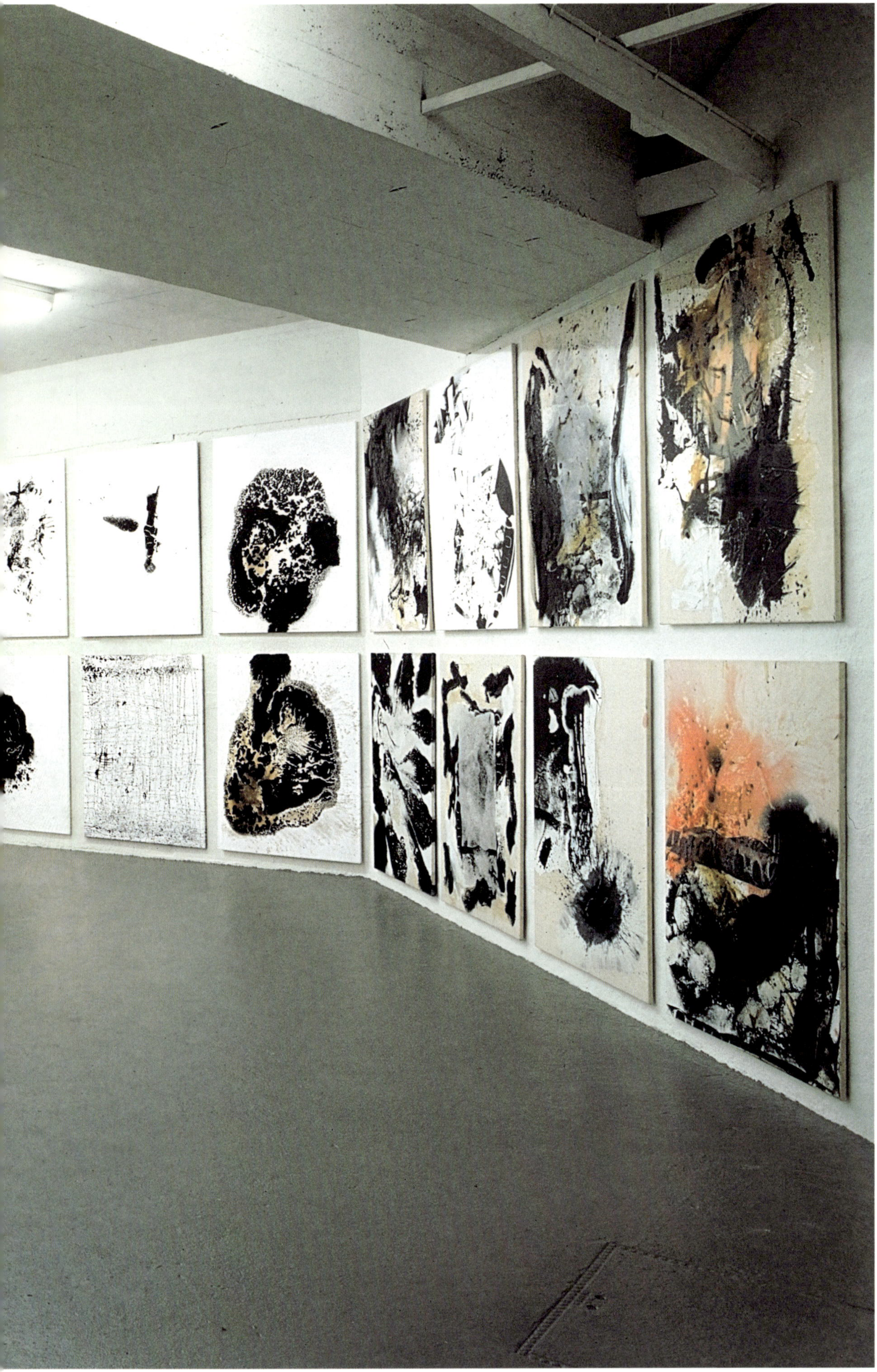

A History of Rocks
1986–1988, Kunstforum,
Städtische Galerie
im Lenbachhaus,
Munich, 1989

the representational space in which McKeever's painterly intervention operates, whereas *A History of Rocks* abstracts and conceptualises that space, impelling what Foucault describes as 'the permanence and uniqueness of an object' to be replaced by 'the space in which various objects emerge and are continuously transformed'[22]. The binary distinction between image and abstraction collapses. Morphological metaphor, graphic diagram, map, and pictorial representation are shown to be among the range of non-categorical modes which a painting can simultaneously adopt.

The title of *A History of Rocks* references geology, among the most empirical of the natural sciences, and one in which hard evidence has provided us with an evolving measure of the earth's age, as well as an ability to posit a relative distinction between 'human time' and 'earth time'. Following the title's suggestion of an empirical methodology, the sequence can be interpreted as a series of experimental combinations of heterogeneous elements, each triggering a reaction which is unforeseeable. The empirical spirit which imbues early British conceptual art, and McKeever's art up to the mid-1980s, is pursued, but subverting its representational basis. McKeever is no longer attempting to discover new means of representing a recalcitrant reality; he is treating representation as one among a potential spectrum of models for reality.

The divorce from representation, and consequently from photography, proposed in *A History of Rocks*, was consolidated in the 'Diptychs' series (1983-90). In the earliest completed works, photographs are almost completely submerged under layers of black paint. In later works – finished in 1990, in time to form the climax of McKeever's mid-career retrospective at the Whitechapel Art Gallery in London – the underlying photograph has been dispensed with altogether.

While *A History of Rocks* proved that McKeever's dialectical method was not contingent upon the binary juxtaposition of alternative forms of representation, the 'Diptychs' test that proposition by placing techniques evolved in his previous series at the service of the binary configuration of the diptych, subverting the template to which they conform. His readoption of the diptych, a form he had returned to episodically throughout the previous two decades, offers the opportunity to take stock of the vicissitudes of his development.

Empirical representation, inherited as a central tenet of the British artistic tradition and a defining characteristic of early British conceptual art, has been jettisoned. The representational model comprehended a reality beyond the work of art, and a moral imperative to be true to it. Even if, for McKeever, the landscape referent was less a subject and more a pretext for a process, or a demarcated terrain in which to base his artistic activity, it provides his work of the 1970s and 80s with a stable destination – literally, in his 'working trips' to remote landscapes; methodologically, as the pictorial space to which the paintings seek access; and psychologically, as a symbolic 'elsewhere' that his painting process strives towards. That the landscapes he visited were relatively unpopulated and unadulterated by human activity suggests an ecological dimension which remains tangential, a by-product rather than an essence. There may be an implicit critique of human interference with the earth's ecological systems but it is never

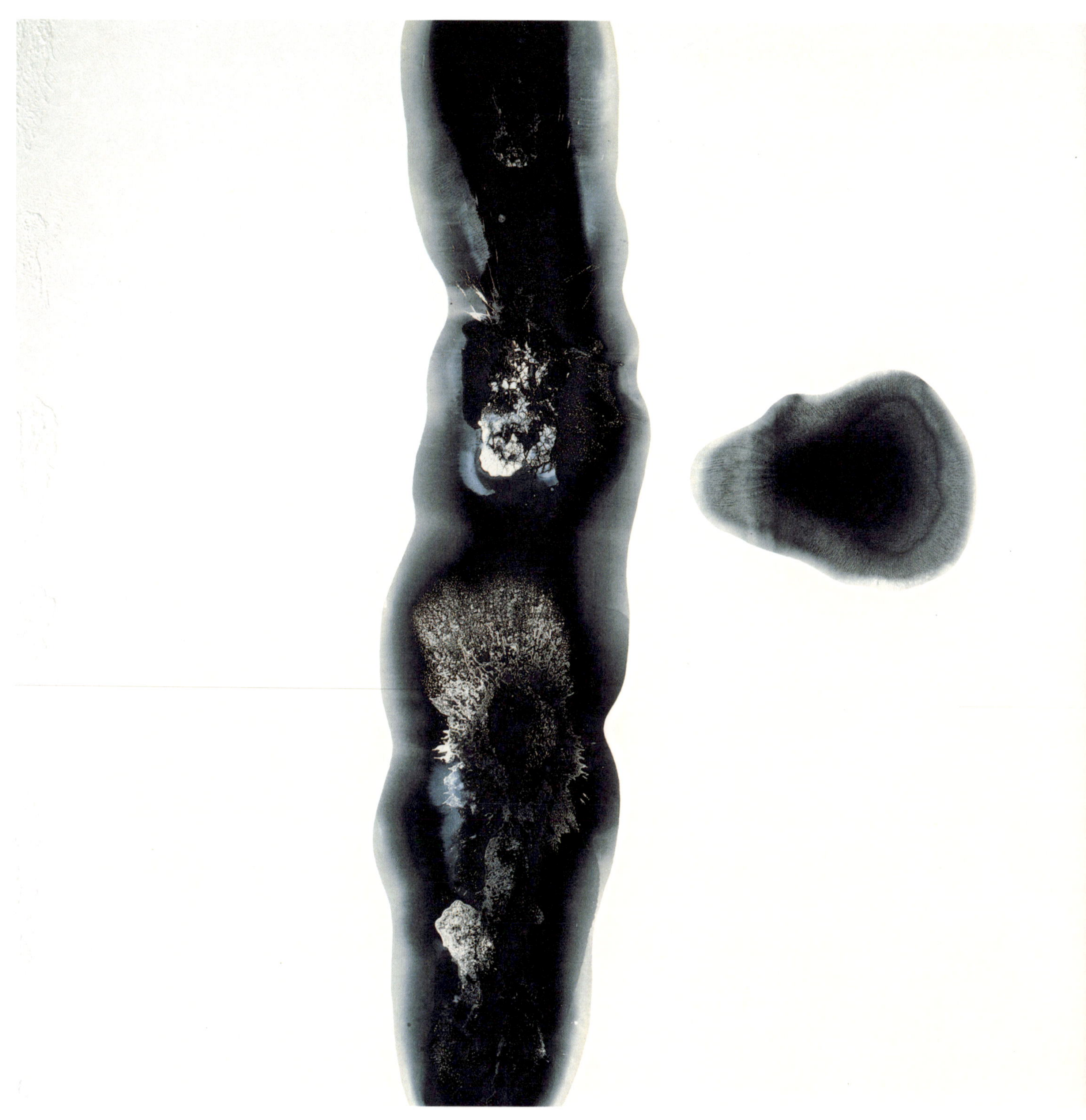

Diptych, FCFN,
1987–1988

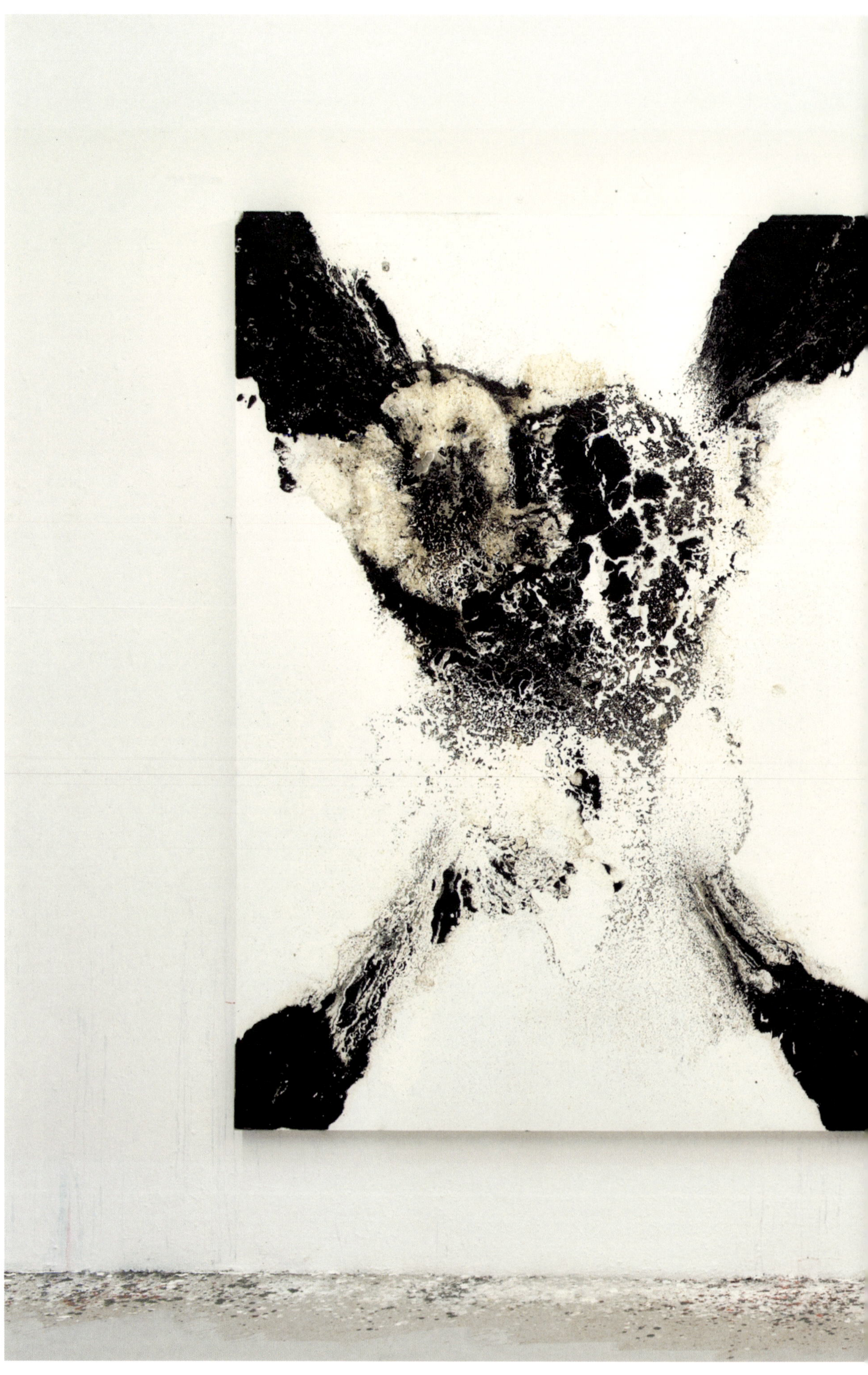

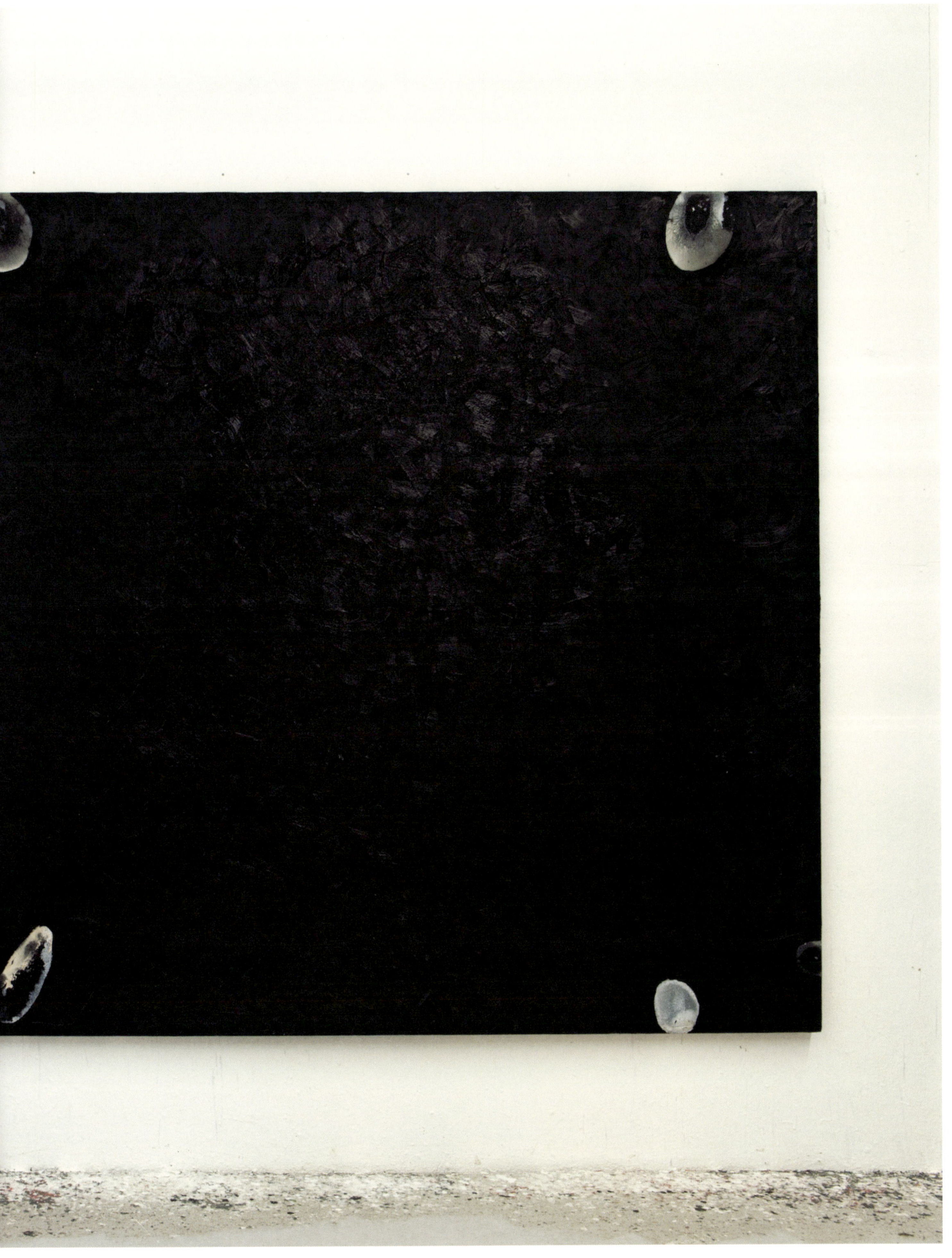

Diptych, Aa II,
1988–1989

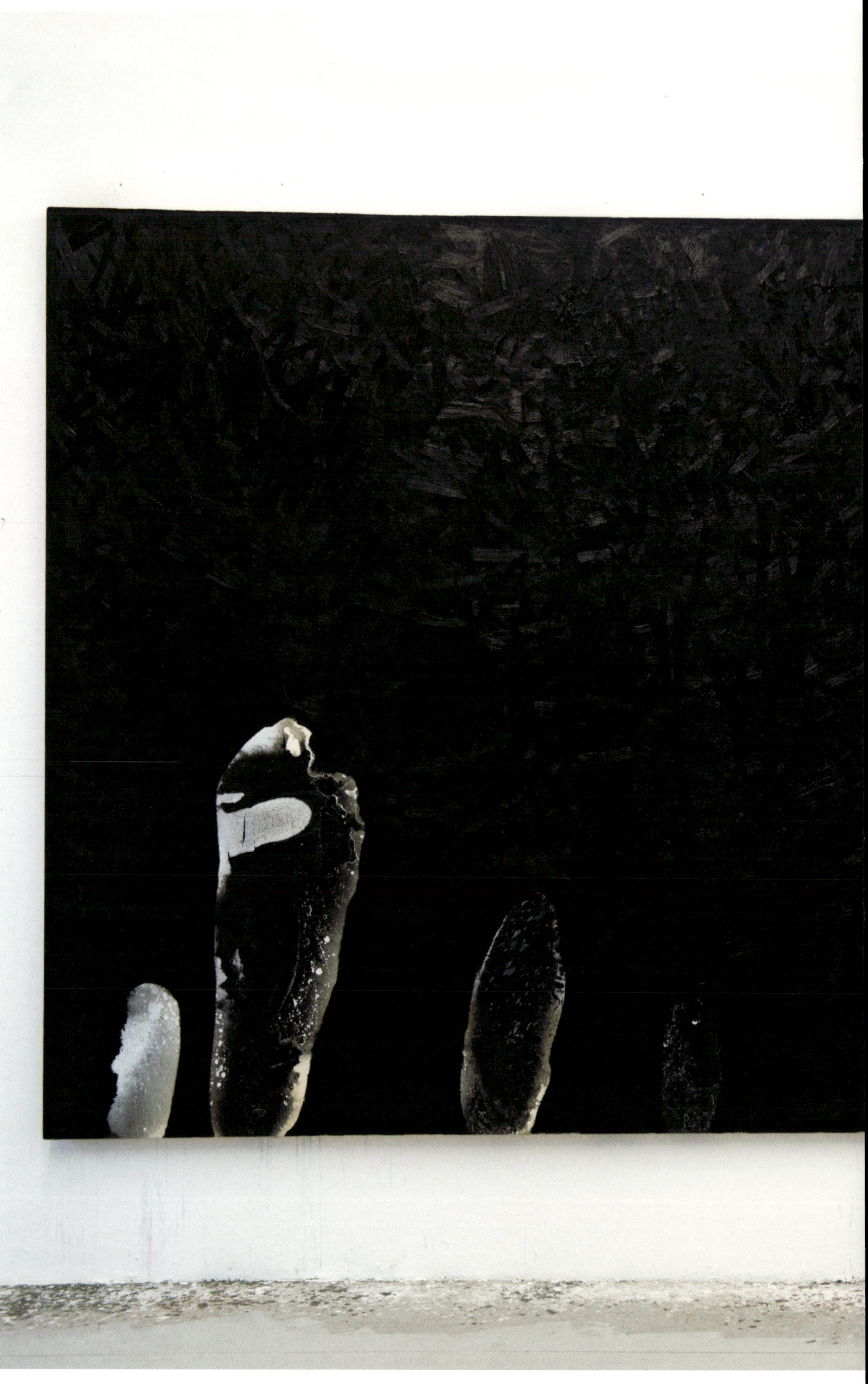

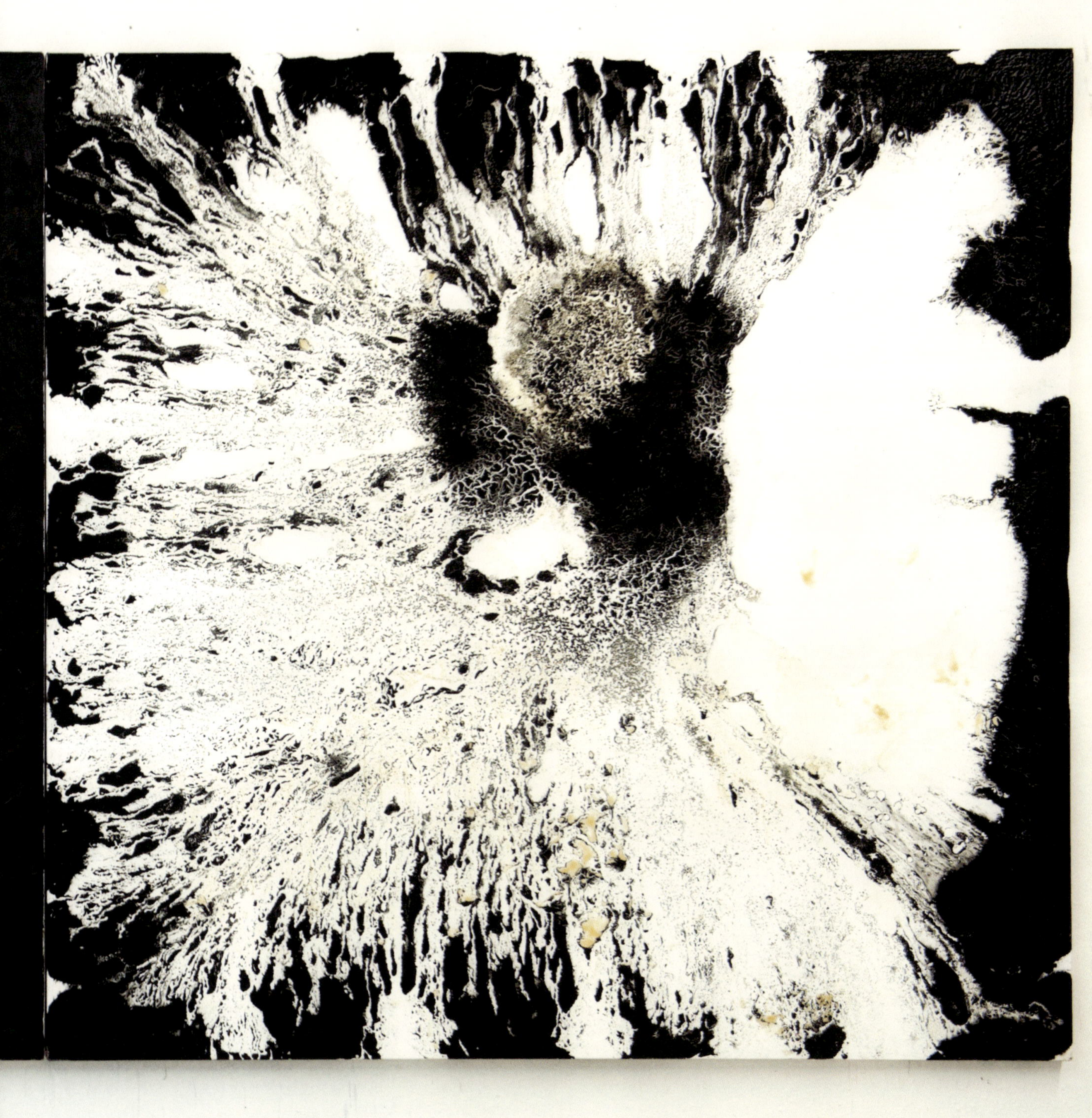

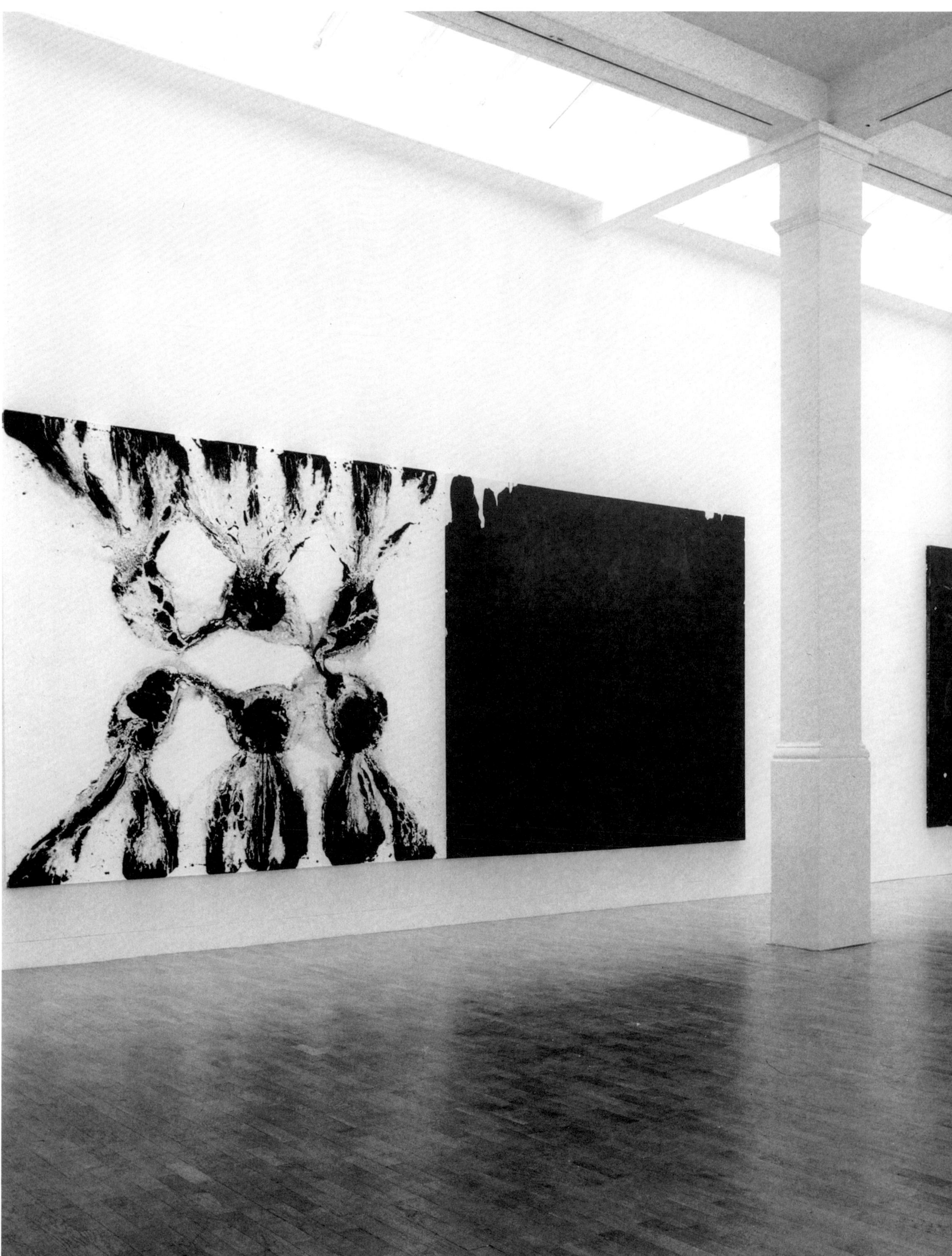

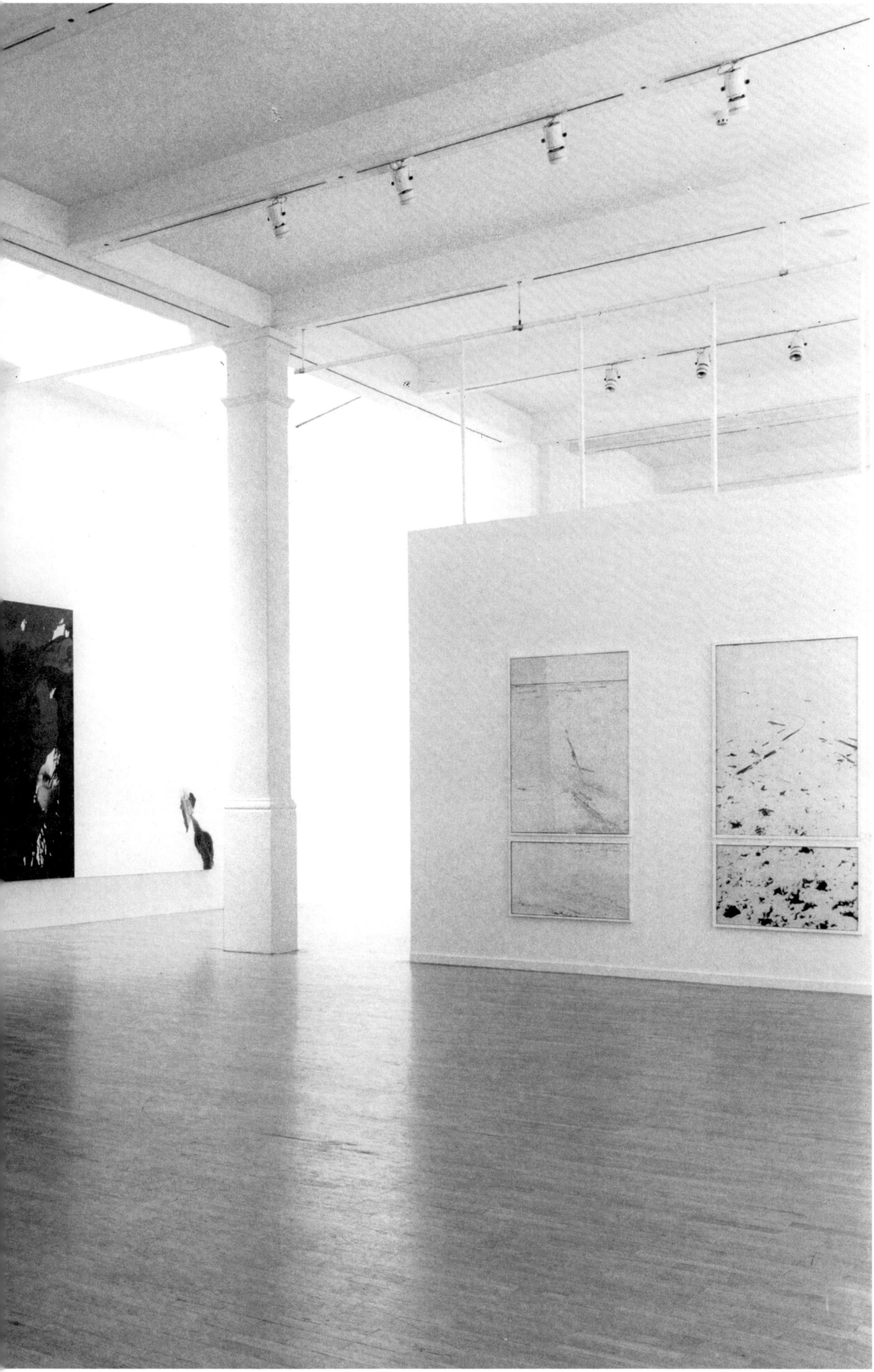

Paintings 1978–1990,
(Diptychs and Field
Series), Whitechapel
Art Gallery, London,
1990

raised to the level of a theme. The secondary significance of the landscape referent corresponds to the predominance McKeever assigns to structuralism over representation. If he inherited both tendencies from early British conceptual art and proceeded to dramatise their incompatibility – the former self-reflexive; the latter outward-looking – the former was always a primary base from which to formulate a critique of the latter.

The 'Diptychs' sublimate the dialectical parameters of McKeever's earlier work – such as those of structuralism and representation – into painterly process, rather than dynamically enacting the relation between them. The diptych form generates a narrative around the various qualities of painting as a medium, such as how it defines an abstract form, and how, unlike photography or graphic illustration, it may simultaneously become formally more specific and representationally more ambiguous. McKeever combines figure-and-ground compositions with those which treat the canvas as a flat area to cover, and holds such contrasting definitions of his activity in equilibrium. Whereas in earlier series the diptych form straddles alternative media, the dualities of the later 'Diptychs' occupy a pure painting context, extrapolating contrasts from within it.

The left panel of *Under the Skin* (1989-90) is dominated by a tall biomorphic form, produced by staining a cotton canvas with black oil paint. Demarcated by the hard, white edge of the background, the gradations of stain suggest the volume of a standing figure but provide no detail to substantiate such a reading. Black oil paint has been poured over the white, primed canvas of the right panel, almost entirely covering its surface except for a few patches which are left exposed, revealing the meandering edges of the black spill like a tide mark. *Under the Skin* contrasts the modelling of abstract form with monochromy, two essential tropes of painterly abstraction. The figural shape dominating the left panel of the diptych recalls and develops similar forms adumbrated in 'Lapland' works, such as the cluster of grey and lilac stains on the right side of *Hearing You Breathe II* (1986), which resemble a ghostly, standing figure.

While *A History of Rocks* can be interpreted as a summary of McKeever's development of the 1970s and 80s, the 'Diptychs' are transitional as well as culminant. Organic processes, such as pouring, seepage and the intermixing of fluid materials which repel each other, produce abstract 'images' which McKeever 'fixes' by isolating them with monochrome fields of flat paint. The photographic connotations of the term 'fixing' are appropriate, as there is a corresponding relation between the flux of natural incident and its freeze in the form of a photographic image. Now that the photographic element is no longer present it has left behind some of its presence in the form of metaphor embodied by painterly process.

If McKeever's paintings, up to and including the 'Lapland' series, have two temporal dimensions – the past and present, held in equilibrium – the 'Diptychs' comprehend those two dimensions while intimating a third: that of potentiality, or futurity, in which the abstract image – which is also an image of the process which created it – is in a state of imaginative becoming. This image carries the viewer forwards and backwards in time, tantalisingly poised in an ambiguous, intermediate space between the process which led to the painting's final state and its potential to have continued onwards from where it was stopped. Abstract formal configurations, such as the six efflorescing nodes which dominate the left panel of *Twice-Doubled* (1989-90), are metaphors for organic form, although they are not pictures of anything. The abstraction of the later 'Diptychs' suggests McKeever's earlier superimposition of gestural painting and photographic image was hybridized, a conflation of pure

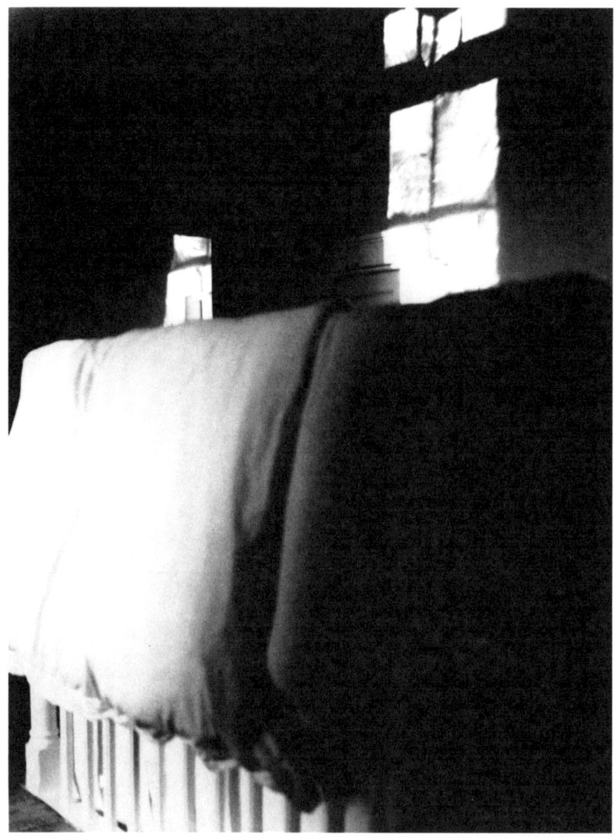

metaphor and the simile of representation. In contrast, the later 'Diptychs' are all material and metaphor, with visible process as their binder.

In later 'Diptychs', such as *Beardmore* (1989-90), the abutting of two canvases relinquishes its relativistic implications, its positing of two distinct interpretations of a single reality, and persists only as a reflexive denial of a categorical statement. White paint has been streamed up and down *Beardmore*'s left panel in translucent tracks that become glossy where the oil paint thickens. In the right panel, the canvas has been stained with black oil paint over which white acrylic was poured while the black was still wet. Swept in vertical tracks across the canvas, the water-based acrylic was tinted by the black oil into which it cannot fully mix. The resulting paint resembles an unhomogenised molten metallic alloy that pools at the bottom edge of the canvas. Contrasting the left and right panels is to see evanescence (left) become explicitness

(right); or a veiled past (left) flowing into an imminent future (right). But these are points in a single narrative, not binary juxtapositions. It is as though the dialectic which had fuelled McKeever's art for two decades had played itself out to leave a potential singularity, a proposition without an alternative upon which it is contingent.

The streaming of paint in parallel tracks across the surface of *Beardmore* looks forward to McKeever's 'Hartgrove Paintings' of the 1990s, in which the singularity of statement intimated by the 'Diptychs' is made manifest. As in much of McKeever's work of the 1980s, most of the series conforms to a method of laying a stained, tonal ground which is subsequently qualified by more defined gestures. But with the absence of the photographic component, these parameters are no longer represented by the two poles of a dialectic between photography and painting, and instead become temporal

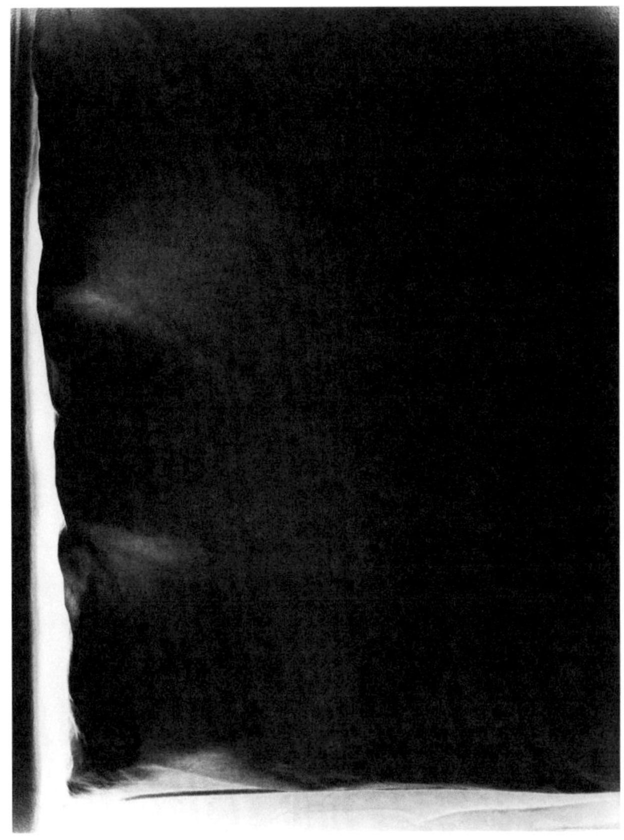

and spatial points in the narrative of a painting process. The time in which paint accretes on the canvas has become synonymous with the expansion of illusionistic space, but not that of a photograph. Painterly gesture has been radically decelerated. Stains of dark oil are overpainted with criss-crossing bands of acrylic which gradually thicken from transparency into opacity, and from matt to gloss. The layering of the paint forms an image of itself, but one from which the trace of individual, painterly handwriting has been removed.

The diptych form of *Beardmore* was an armature for a dialectical relation which McKeever had developed to accommodate a conceptual contrast between painting and photography. Relieved of supporting that dialectic, it remained as a refutation of a categorical statement more than a positive assertion. It would take the reappearance of the photograph in McKeever's art to reactivate that dialectic, and that did not occur until twenty years later, in 2010, when McKeever exhibited a series of black-and-white photographs at the Royal Academy of Arts in London, alongside a selection of the 'Hartgrove Paintings'[23]. Subsequently he has extended the reintegration of photography into his practice in the 'Eagduru' and 'Against Architecture' series (both 2011–13).

The 'Hartgrove Photographs' (2007–10) are high-contrast black-and white bromide prints, approximately 20 cm wide, depicting details of the interior of McKeever's home (Hartgrove is the name of the small hamlet to which the house belongs). The surrounding landscape is not visible, although its light can be intuited: in a cruciform of white bleeding from a gridwork of blinds; or from a series of pale, aqueous panels of brilliance cast onto the wall at the turn of a staircase. The patterns that arise from the interplay of light and shadow are abstractions that conceal or veil the body of the house.

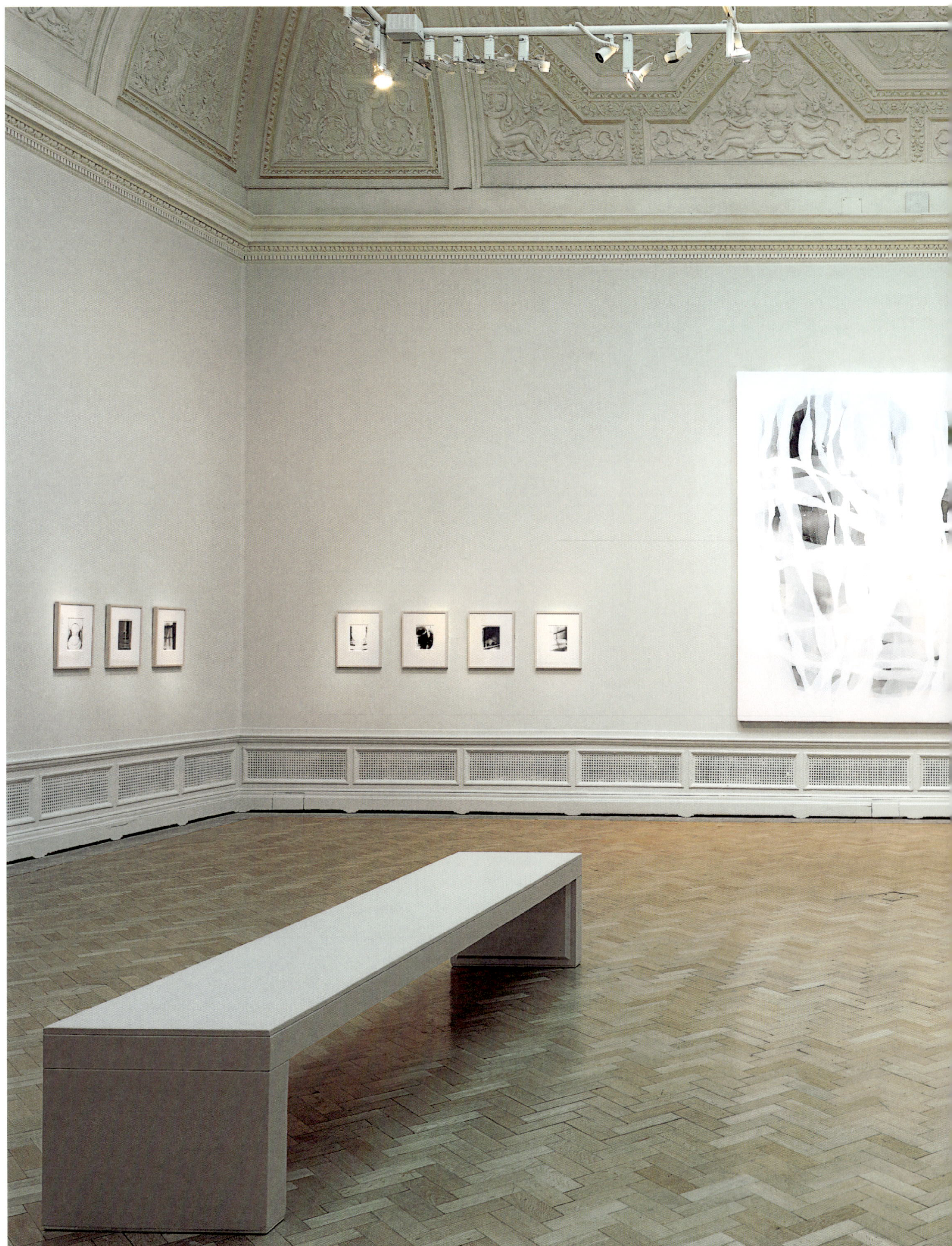

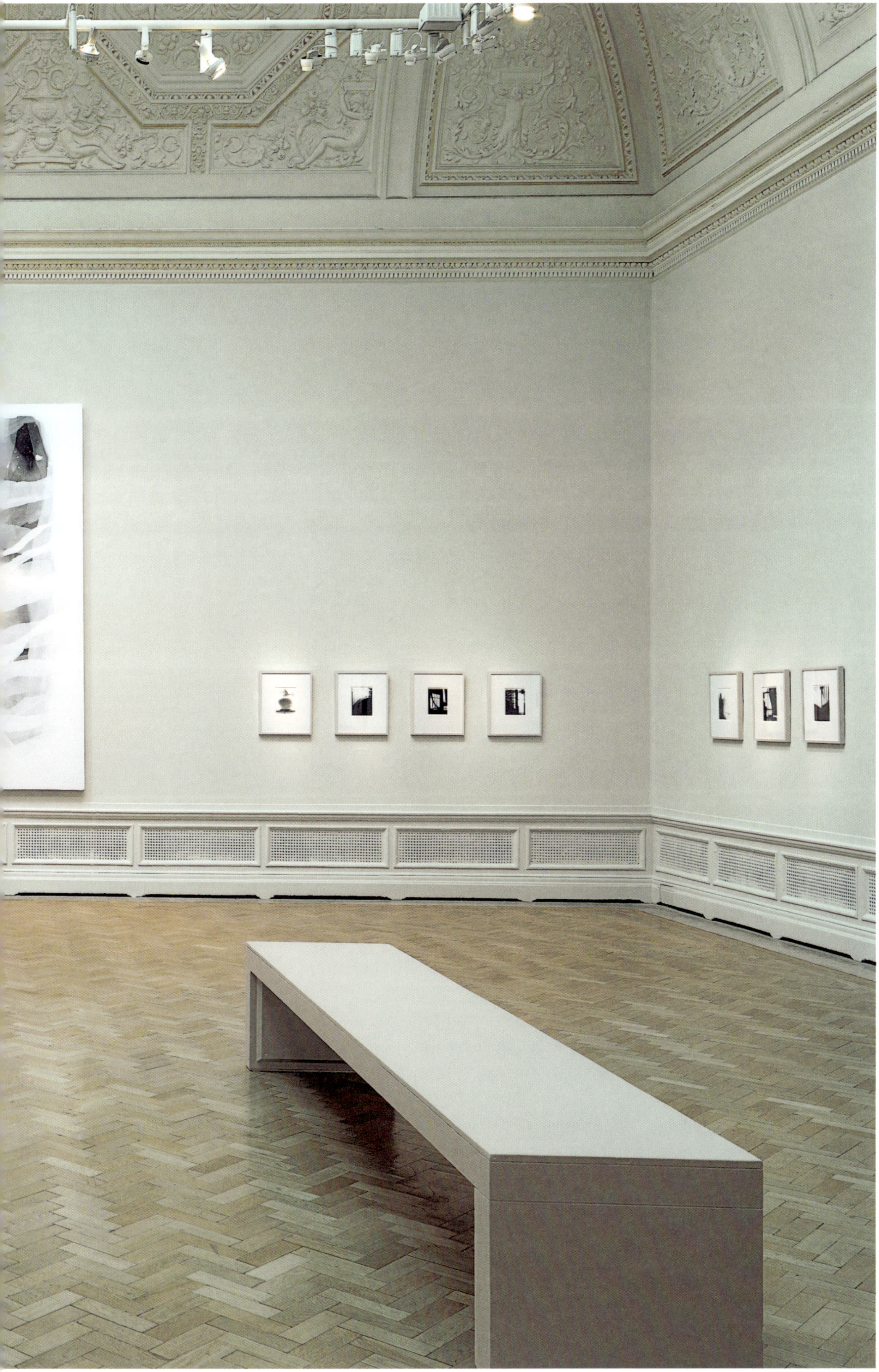

Artists' Laboratory:
Ian McKeever RA,
(Hartgrove Painting
and Photographs),
Royal Academy of
Arts, London, 2010

Here, photographic image is less a representation of a material reality than a conduit from which that reality can be inferred. The dynamic by which abstractions both resist our access to a represented reality and draw us towards it makes McKeever's photographic method in the 'Hartgrove Photographs' correspond to his painting process in the 'Hartgrove Paintings', in which translucent veils of colour appear to recede towards the tonal gradations of a stained canvas ground.

The 'Eagduru' and 'Against Architecture' series[24] contain similar photographs, but they have been left unframed, mounted onto plywood, and cropped so narrowly that the already-attenuated representation of 'The Hartgrove Photographs' is rendered almost abstract. Most of the works from either series are approximately 50cm high, a relatively small scale within McKeever's oeuvre, inclining the viewer to approach a work as a pictorial window rather than a physical object to be confrontedBut the works themselves resist this expectation. Only the photographic half of *Eagduru 15* (2013) explicitly reveals itself as an image: of sunlight falling onto fabric, while the pale square hovering above it is a window. Otherwise, the pronounced objecthood of the works asserts itself against an image-orientated reading.

The deceptive correspondences that *Eagduru 21* (2013) develops between painting and photography take us back to McKeever's 'Waterfalls' series. A first glance suggests the symmetry of two abutting sections. Each features a dominant grey or white shape, narrowing from top to bottom, and flanked on the outside by an uneven border in a contrasting tone. Morphological symmetry encourages an assumption of likeness; but closer scrutiny reveals that the right half is a black-and-white photograph, and the left a painting, and that the white border along the right edge

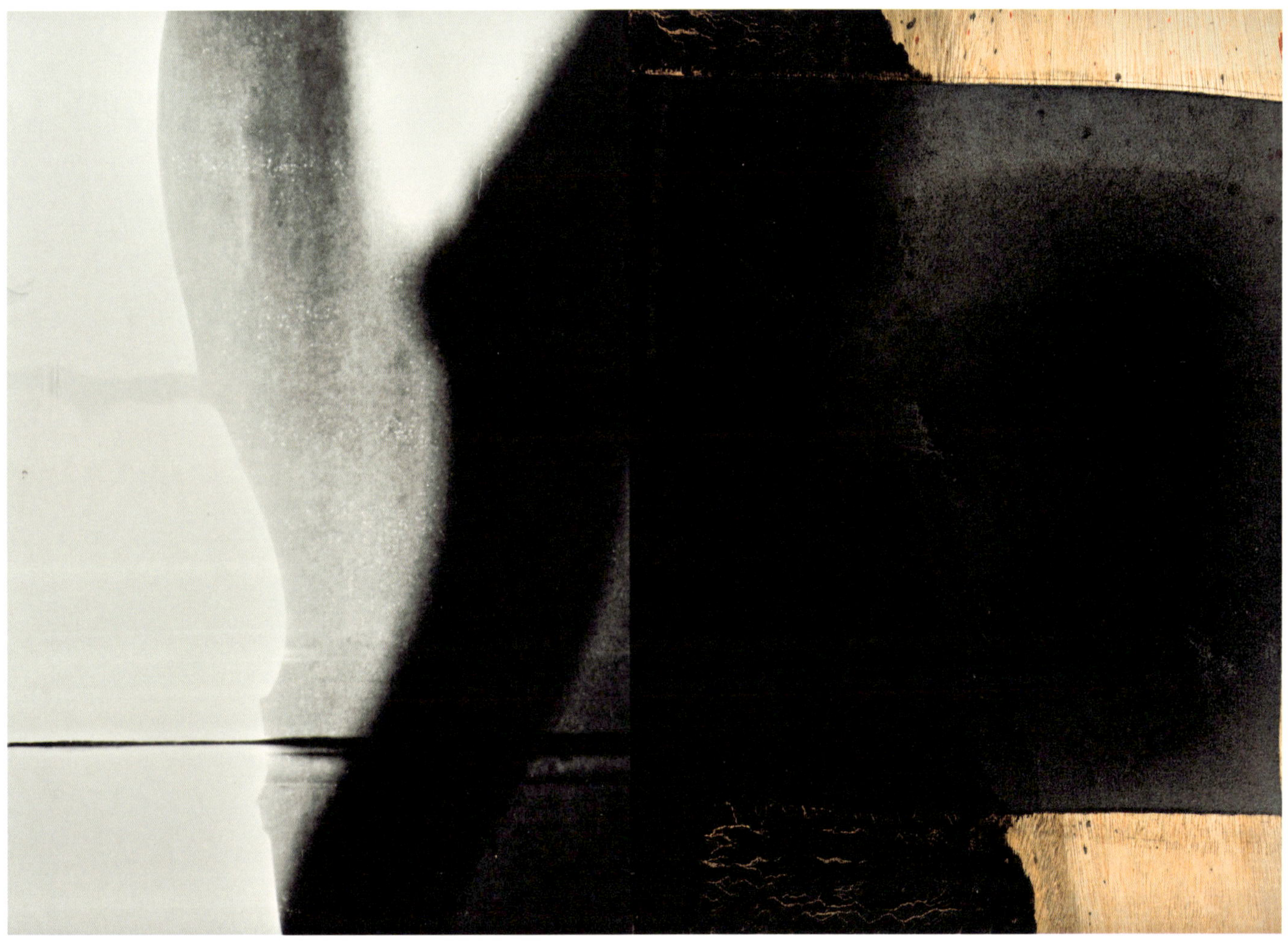

of the work's photographic half is an image of a clump of fabric, possibly a duvet or a cushion, over a flat area of grey fabric. A piece of cotton canvas has been affixed to the raw plywood ground of the left half, leaving a raw plywood margin exposed. White paint only partially covers this canvas, forming a shape that roughly corresponds to the area of exposed grey fabric in the photograph, as the brown margin of wood symmetrically reflects the white of the duvet. These formal correspond-ences work to erode the otherness of photographic image and abstract painting, and insist on symmetry.

In his essay *Art and Objecthood* (1967), the modernist critic Michael Fried simultaneously celebrated US modernist painting and resisted its demise by articulating a critique of Minimal Art, such as the work of Robert Morris and Donald Judd, which he calls 'literalist art'. For Fried, the device of shape in modernist painting was a means of resisting art's reduction to mere object, a condition he saw Minimal Art

as embodying. He wrote, 'What is at stake in this conflict is whether the paintings or objects in question are experienced as paintings or as objects: and what decides their identity as *painting* is their confronting of the demand that they hold as shapes. Otherwise they are experienced as nothing more than objects. This can be summed up by saying that modernist painting has come to find it imperative that it defeat or suspend its own objecthood, and that the crucial factor in this undertaking is shape, but shape that must belong to *painting* – not, or not merely, literal.'[25] Fried comprehends shape as capable of being both pictorial, and therefore object-denying, and materialistic, and therefore object-declaring; and he is clearly in favour of the former.

Eagduru 21 develops a dialectical relation between these positions. The photographic element claims the medium of shape for illusion, counter-designating the painting's corresponding shapes as mere object. But these definitions are

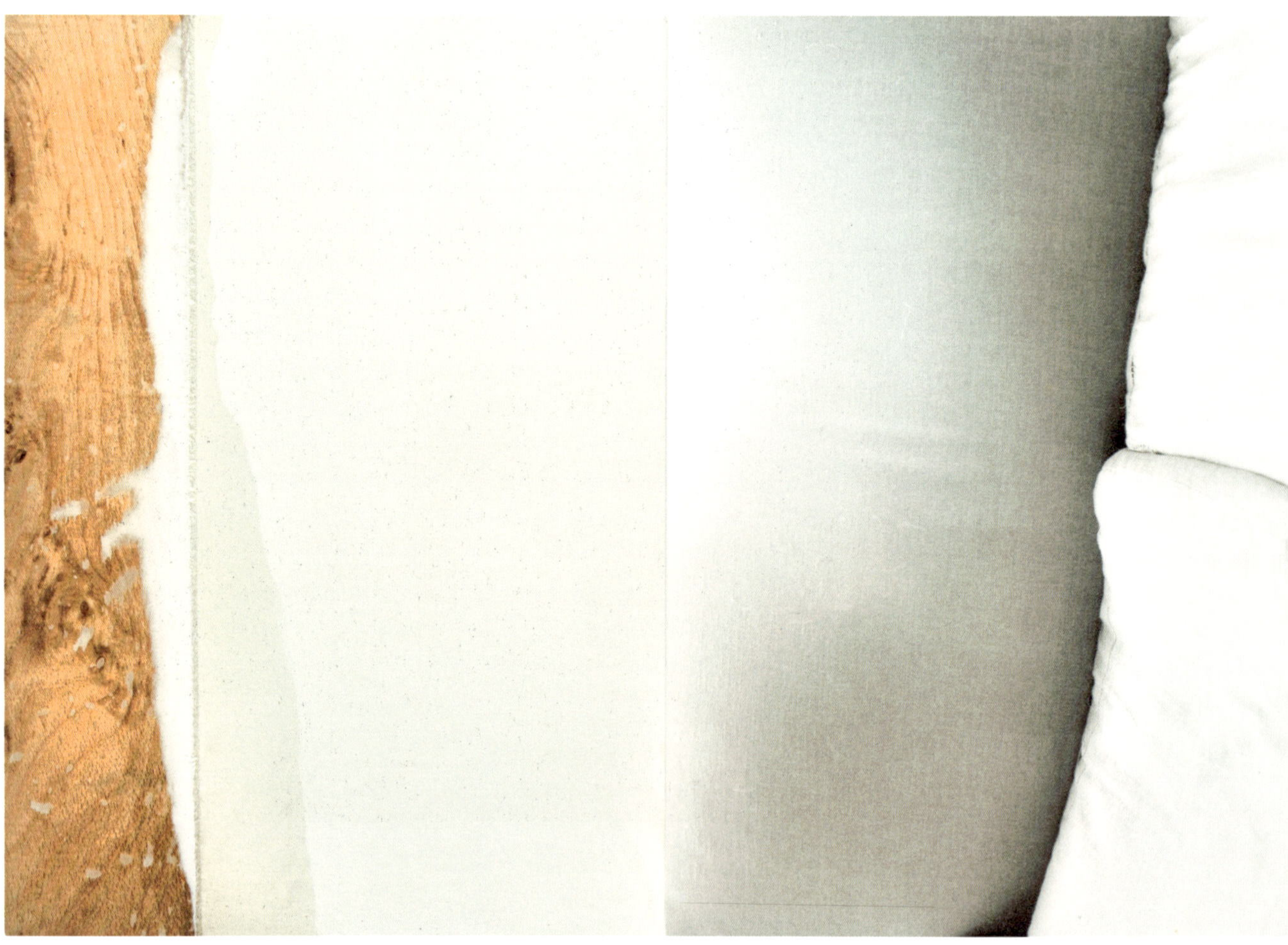

unstable: in comparison with the literalness of photography – literal in the sense of its essentially representational function, however ambiguous McKeever's cropping makes its referent – the shapes articulated by painting can be seen as less reductive to an object, in the sense of a referent. Painting is shown to be liberated into spatial and perceptual ambiguities of the sort Fried was promoting. It shakes itself loose of the object which the photograph is limited to signifying. And yet, an antithetical reading is just as apparent and valid. The photograph is all illusion, object-evading – in the sense that its illusion distracts us from its material vehicle – while the painting is mere object, manifestly declaring its material constituents. Neither reading is allowed to become categorical, to hold its ground. The relativism between them remains in a dynamic suspension which is bridged, as often in McKeever's art, by the lightest of visual puns: between the fabric of the canvas which is the white paint's ground, and

the fabric of the bedsheet which is the photograph's subject. It is as if the perfunctoriness of this simple correspondence had the function of advising us that the work's true narrative lies on another level, and of directing us to it by default.

Fried's text was written on the cusp between USA late modernism and the era of postmodern relativism which was succeeding it. The new Minimal Art he rejected was itself conflicted, with one foot still caught in the modernist aesthetics out of which it emerged. The dialectic between modernist autonomy and relativism has also been McKeever's central narrative.

The 'Eagduru' series places an abstract painting and a black-and-white photograph – each upright rectangles – side-by-side, connoting the photograph/painting pairings of McKeever's work of the 1970s and 80s. But the seam between the two halves of *Eagduru 21* has a more ambiguous function than the corresponding division between the two panels of

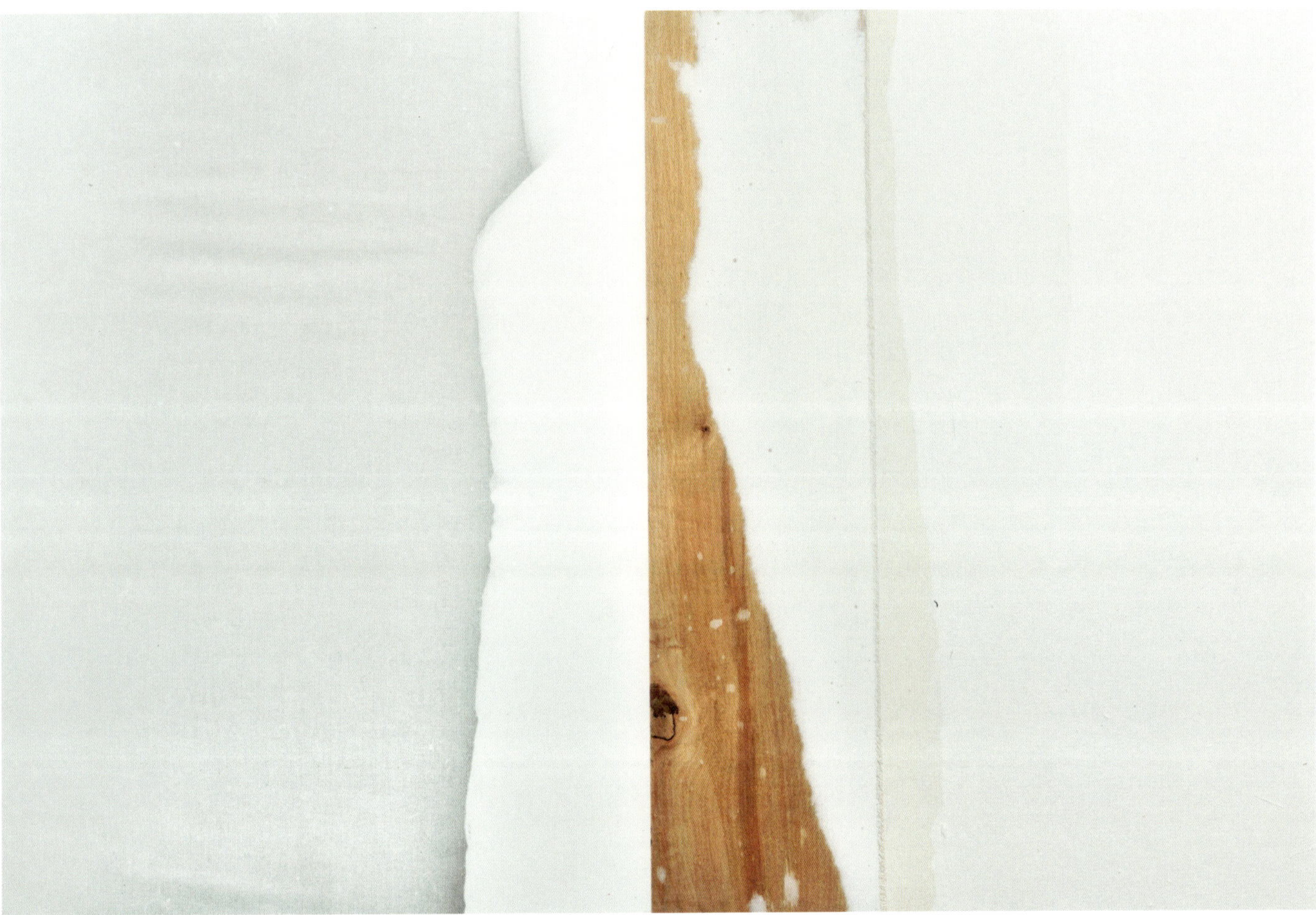

a 'Waterfalls' diptych. The relative symmetry between the halves makes it a spatial parting, like a Barnett Newman 'zip', as well as a division between two alternative media. It is both a relativistic force field and a modernist juncture. McKeever's earlier dialectic between media has been sublimated to that between textures and shapes that only secondarily register as those of a photograph or a painting. A shadow becomes a stain; the varying depths of each transferred, by association, onto the other. The rigid surfaces of photographic paper or painted canvas, when affixed to wood, become charged thresholds. The extent to which they will succumb to illusion is the drama around which the series moves; hence its title, from an Anglo-Saxon word meaning 'window', or literally 'eye-door', implying the paradigmatic shift from surface to space, and from materiality to illusion.

The 'Against Architecture' series splinters the photographic image even more radically, forcing it to submit to constructivistic configurations. Many of the works are composed of more than two elements, arranged on top of each other as well as side-by-side. Blocks of pure, painted colour abut or surmount photographic fragments. The edges of the plywood supports produce odd, organic, slightly off-rectangular shapes and uneven junctures. Image is constrained to a tonal strip; painting to a block or band of solid, primary colour. As with 'Eagduru', the title 'Against Architecture' is telling, directing us to the constructivism of the works as to its fissuring by the insubstantiality of the photographic image. The images are so frustrated by their crop, and by the dominant objecthood of their supports, that they are unable to signify more than material succumbing to illusion. But this sense of unmanifested illusionism refutes a reductive reading of the works as purely formalistic compositions. The photographs puncture the tiled configurations with a sense of spatial potential which subverts their insistent materiality.

Abstraction, which has previously functioned, in McKeever's art, as a metaphor for how reality is perceived, here begins to assume the role of a model for how reality might be ordered: composed of both concrete materiality and imaginative speculation. The compositions resemble standing stone structures, and similarly hint at an order whose rationale, although evident, remains mysterious.

The 'Against Architecture' series converts the lure of the photographic image, which McKeever's art of the 1980s offset with the physical immediacy of painting, into bricks kicked out of a putative constructivism. The solidity of architecture and the insubstantiality of illusionistic space each has its own directional dynamic: building upwards, or drawing us into its depths. Placed in close conjunction, these dynamics merge into their shared role as building blocks within a compositional structure which transcends their differences. The soft blacks and whites of photographic tonality are supplied with hard edges by their plywood supports, to aid their assimilation by the hard-edged colours of plywood stained with oil paint. The differences in medium blend into aspects of a tiled, multi-textured surface. It is the junctures between the constituent elements which create the works' defining, constructivistic order, as if the tensions of McKeever's dialectic between painting and photography, in which each medium asserted its relative primacy as a vehicle for representing experience, had been resolved into the space between them, which is that of neither.

Notes

1   'the test … function': F. Scott
    Fitzgerald, *The Crack-Up,* Edited
    by Edmund Wilson, New
    Directions Publishing, New York,
    2009, p.69

2   'too messy … painters': quoted
    from a conversation with the
    author, 28.11.13.

3   'the inaugural .. art': Patricia
    Bickers, *Art Monthly 1976-: On
    the gentle art of staying the same
    while changing utterly,* Art
    Libraries Journal, 2010, p.5.

4   'was very much … painters': Ibid.,
    p.10.

5   'the neatness … painter': from an
    unpublished letter to the author,
    dated 29.11.13.

6   'I remember … painting': Ian
    McKeever, *Black and White …
    Or How to Paint with a Hammer,*
    Matts Gallery, London, 1982.

7   ⁷'I think … activity': from an
    interview with Tony Godfrey,
    published in *Fields, Waterfalls,
    and Birds – Ian McKeever,* Arnolfini,
    Bristol, 1980.

8   'unintelligible': Roland Barthes,
    The Reality Effect, in *French
    Literary Theory Today,* ed. Tzvatan
    Todorov (Cambridge: Cambridge
    University Press, 1982), p.14

9   'an act … cool logic': from an
    unpublished letter to the author,
    dated 29.11.13.

10 'that-has-been': Roland Barthes,
    Camera Lucida (trans. Richard
    Howard), London: Vintage,
    2000, p.96.

11 'the existing … the new': T.S Eliot,
    Selected Prose, UK.: Penguin Books,
    1965, p.23.

12 'Poetry … personality': Ibid., p. 29.

13 *Borderlines – Abstracting Art from
    Nature,* Arnolfini, Bristol, 1985
    (with Frank Auerbach).

14 'to bring … violently': David
    Sylvester, *The Brutality of Fact:
    Interviews with Francis Bacon,*
    London, 1975, p.12.

15 'I don't … upon you': Ibid., p.65.

16 'When I was … to record': Ibid., p.17.

17 'like … subject': from a
    conversation with the author, 1986.

18 'painting … space': Ian McKeever,
    *Notes around a Painting for a Hole
    in the Ground,* Aspects, no.10,
    September 1978.

19 'We shall … itself': Michel Foucault,
    The Archaeology of Knowledge,
    Tavistock Publications, London,
    1972, p.48.

20 'to dispense … things': Ibid., p.47.

21 'the embrace … things': Ibid., p.49.

22 'the permanence … object'; 'the
    space … transformed': Ibid., p.32.

23 *Artists' Laboratory 01: Ian McKeever
    RA,* Royal Academy of Arts, London,
    8 September–24 October, 2010.

24 These two series were first
    exhibited in the exhibition *Ian
    McKeever: Eagduru and Against
    Architecture,* Galleri Susanne
    Ottesen, Copenhagen, 28
    February–5 April, 2014.

25 'What is … literal': Michael Fried,
    Art and Objecthood: Artforum,
    June 1967.

pp.4–5
Drawing for proposed 'grass verge painting' for a wood, July 1975
Graphite, crayon, gouache and photograph on paper
54.5 × 80 cm

p.8
Study for 'Painting for a Hole in the Ground', 1977
Graphite and crayon on paper, collaged with gouache on paper
74 × 105 cm

p.9
Study for 'Painting for a Hole in the Ground', 1977
Graphite and crayon on paper, collaged with gouache on paper
74 × 105 cm

p.14
Sand and Sea Series No.6, Withernsea, East Yorkshire, Spring 1977
Graphite on paper and photographs
99 × 152 cm

p.15
Sand and Sea Series No.8, Withernsea, East Yorkshire, Spring 1977
Graphite on paper and photographs
99 × 152 cm

pp.16–17
Sand and Sea Series No.5, Withernsea, East Yorkshire, Spring 1977
Graphite on paper and photographs
99 × 152 cm

pp.22–28
Field Series, 1978 (12 individual works)
Each work in two parts.
Upper panel: Graphite on paper
Lower panel: Photograph
195 × 93 cm

p.36
Waterfalls No.2, 1979
Left panel: Silver gelatine print
Right panel: Charcoal, pastel and acrylic on paper
152.4 × 182.9 cm

p.37
Waterfalls No.3, 1979
Left panel: Silver gelatine print
Right panel: Pastel on paper
152.4 × 172.7 cm

p.38–39
Waterfalls No.5, 1979
Left panel: Charcoal, pastel, graphite and acrylic on paper
Right panel: Silver gelatine print
152.4 × 203.2 cm

p.40–41
Waterfalls No.1, 1979
Left panel: Silver gelatine print
Right panel: Charcoal and pastel on paper
155 × 222.5 cm

p.42–43
Waterfalls No.7, 1979
Left panel: Silver gelatine print
Right panel: Charcoal and pastel on paper
152.4 × 223.5cm

p.48
Night Flak: The evening dawn shows grey, 1981
Left panel: Oil on canvas
Right panel: Pastel and charcoal on paper
213 × 305 cm

p.49
Night Flak: A night of solace in the dark of fears, 1981
Left panel: Oil on canvas
Right panel: Pastel and charcoal on paper
213 × 305 cm

p.54
TL 13 Early Morning – The Needles, 1983
Oil and photograph on canvas
250 × 164 cm

p.56–57
TL 9 Earth of the Slumbering and Liquid Trees, 1983
Oil and photograph on canvas
213 × 310 cm

p.58
Night Snow I, 1985
Oil and photograph on canvas
220 × 170 cm

p.61
TL 11 Beside the Brambled Ditch, 1983
Oil and photograph on canvas
230 × 208 cm

p.63
Towards Night, 1984
Oil and photograph on canvas
220 × 230 cm

imprint

Published by HackelBury Fine Art, London.

An irregular periodical dedicated to the work
of a single artist; in-depth and in print.

imprint #1
July 2014

e: imprint@hackelbury.co.uk
t: +44 (0)20 7937 8688

HackelBury Fine Art Ltd
4 Launceston Place
London W8 5RL

For issue and subscription details:
www.hackelbury.co.uk/imprint

Editor: Kate Stevens
Production: Phil Crook
Production Assistant: Bridie Riley
Project Assistance: Judy Adam

Design: Victoria Forrest
www.designbyvictoria.com

Printed in Italy
2000 copies
Printed on Munken Lynx Rough

ISSN 2055-5431 / ISBN 978-0-9570263-1-5